Sourcebook of
FAMILY HUMOR

Sourcebook of
FAMILY
HUMOR

OREN ARNOLD

KREGEL PUBLICATIONS
Grand Rapids, Michigan 49501

Library of Congress Catalog Card Number 79-92503
ISBN 0-8254-2106-3

Printed in the United States of America

Introduction

Give your home a sense of humor. Through the following pages, we have great fun joking, sharing life's humor with one another. It is not the intention of the author to "laugh at" family humor situations, but to encourage families to laugh together—to share a natural, spontaneous sense of humor. For family relationships, "humor" is actually a "serious" business. In 1970, *Home Life* published an article under the above title which explained and illustrated my views on the necessity of family humor. With the permission of that publication, I have included some portions of the article here. I do this because I believe that for happy, successful family living, any couple must develop an abiding sense of humor in themselves and in their children.

The importance of this cannot be overemphasized. True, it is not a revolutionary fact; it has been here forever. But it has remained tragically unrecognized. There has been a tendency to push humor back, as somehow being in conflict with sacred things. Some so-called authorities, if they consider humor at all, consider it as inconsequential. A recent perusal of some two dozen volumes on marriage and family relations, including both sociological and religious treatments, failed to uncover a single significant treatment of humor, not even a suggestion that humor has a place, much less an important place, in family relationships. Yet isn't it interesting that the most widely read comic strips (Blondie, Family Circus,

Dennis the Menace, Peanuts, for example) all deal with humor in the family situation! These are humorous because they reflect clearly the family situations we have all experienced. They are neither forced nor artificial—they let us laugh at ourselves. They represent the very spontaneity which is the essence of family humor.

We could say the same for the long-running TV programs. Among those which have the longest records of high rating are the family situation comedies. We are attracted to these representations of family humor because of the reality they portray.

The first kind of humor which characterizes or can contribute to a comfortable family situation is spontaneous, original humor. Some of this is so spontaneous in children as to be almost accidental. For example, consider the Patrick O'Reilly home. Recently, the O'Reilly's were having a party, and one of the several adult guests, admiring the house, happened to ask twelve-year-old Robin if her father had a den.

"No," said Robin, eyes glowing, "Pop just growls all over the house."

Papa Patrick might well have scolded her for being so smarty—if we hearken to the disciplinarians. Pop thought not. "She was being one of us; she felt a companionship with us grownups," said he, later. "I am happy that she did. After all, her mother and I make many a joke at her expense, playing and having family fun. Robin was not being impertinent. She was really asking for acceptance as one of our happy group."

Robin is more fortunate than millions of youngsters. Adult maturity or lack of it is never revealed more surely than in the reaction to "insult humor" such as Robin pulled on her father. When he growled big and pretended to chase her in anger, the whole party was enlivened and somehow, warmed.

Another example is seen in five-year-old Kathy Veldt responding to Mama's "Please pass the salt, Kathy," by passing the pepper shaker and waiting innocently to burst into beautiful laughter when mama failed to discover the switch until shaking out some pepper on her vegetables. These are examples of unplanned humor; they result from the right combination of circumstances, people and conversation. To deny children the freedom of this kind of spontaneous expression is to rob the family of a significant part of that which will contribute to binding the family together.

Another type of family humor is the "semi-planned" humor. The family member (often a child) who uses this, converts a situation or experience occurring at one time and place into humor at another time and place. Sometimes it is carefully thought out—but more often it is only a subconscious thought until the inspiration of the right moment. For example, young Randy Detwiler reported one evening, "Dad, one of the fellows at school said I look like you."

Proud Dad beamed and said, "Ah! And what did you say then?"

"Nothing," replied Randy, grinning and edging away. "He's bigger than I am."

Again, the father pretended anger at the child, and young Randy was delighted; he sensed that his Dad's good humor was spontaneous.

Some of these humor situations occur in the application of a joke heard outside the home to a situation inside the home. Dr. William McGrath, a Psychiatrist friend shared one of these situations from his home. One morning before school he said to fourteen-year-old Jane, "Pick up your room."

"I can't," she shot back. "It's too heavy."

Jane was at what is often called (at best) a troublesome age. But she was merely "reaching for adulthood" as her father admits now. At the moment, Dr. McGrath was as human as the next father. His reaction was to kick at the family dog and snarl, "I won't have levity around this house!"

Whereupon a smiling bright-eyed Janie stuck her lovely

head back in the door and called to the dog, "Here, Levity, here Levity, nice dog!" then ran off to school.

Another experience from about twenty-one years ago found a father (whose watch had failed) calling home and asking, "What time does the clock say there?"

Son Richard (claiming he didn't recognize father's voice) responded, "It doesn't say anything—you have to look at it."

In spite of his frustration with the watch and his immediate anxiety over the time, father responded with genuine laughter, recognizing that his question had "set him up" for the answer.

In either of these examples, the father could have responded with real anger or with accusations of "Smart Aleck!", but either of these responses would have inserted an unhealthy note into a situation which could aid "family health."

The third area of family humor is the structured, the planned (sometimes elaborately planned) joke. In some families this involves the sending of "gag" birthday or anniversary greeting cards and then watching for the expression and reaction when the envelope is opened. In other cases it may involve baking a "surprise" into favorite cookies or cakes.

One father recalls his sudden embarrassing anger at his eleven-year-old Gail when she sewed up the tops of his new socks. "But who short-sheeted my bed last week, Daddy?" she cried, appalled at his reaction. He had to hug the child and say he was only pretending to be mad. Truly, any parent teaching a tolerant sense of humor simultaneously develops his own.

There are many facets of each of these types, of course, but these categories cover the types of family humor which are most helpful in establishing and maintaining good interpersonal relationships among family members.

One of the reasons we should encourage family humor is that humor is a very natural phenomenon. From the very early self entertainment of children through the sense of the comic and on to the sophistication of puns and wit, humor is a part of being human. In fact, as the psychiatrist Martin Grotjahn points out in his book *BEYOND LAUGHTER* (McGraw-Hill, 1957), laughter is strictly a human phenomenon. He writes, "Animals cannot smile and do not laugh." Children laugh naturally—from exhuberance—and so should adults. Humor is something to delight in—to enjoy. The big laugh is not essential. A truly good sense of humor is a quieter blessing, a concomitant of poise and peace of mind. The smile is better evidence of a sense of humor than is the belly-laugh.

But the fact that humor is natural to man does not mean it is always present. The intelligent adult will encourage the facets of humor which seem instinctive, lest the feeling for humor dry up—die away. "It must be guided, stimulated, and constantly used," my friend Dr. McGrath tells me. Humor is not trivial, frothy nothingness, as some would claim. It can actually add "gracenotes" to all our living. We should seek to stimulate and develop it in its natural spontaneity.

Another reason to encourage family humor is for its therapeutic effect. In the normal family, the strain of interpersonal relationships often produces a heaviness, an atmosphere of wariness or of hurt. Love becomes hidden behind personal pride and the coldness of temporary spats. In the home where humor is "alive and well" tensions can be broken and love quickly brought again into evidence through natural humor. An appreciative smile or gesture, a tone of good will, a quick chuckle—this is the rewarding atmosphere. Its opposite is a chip-on-the-shoulder glumness, or a tight-lipped seriousness. A haughty hostility that blights all of family life. Many is the time when little Kathy Veldt, in the immediate tension of parent-child or parent-parent crisis— even if the disappointment or scolding words were directed at her, has climbed up and kissed Dad on the nose or on his bald head, smiled and said, "I love you" and turned a tense moment into great humor and pleasure. Humor is contagious—let *it* spread in place of the interpersonal tensions which can stifle love. In an atmosphere of loving good nature, blight cannot thrive.

Of course there are forms of so-called humor which can hurt a family, rather than help. The overbearing tease, the embarrassing or insulting practical joke, the joke which degrades a family member or capitalizes on a handicap or weakness—these are all dangerous. Parents should be careful never to use these forms and to discourage—to prevent their use by the children. Other so-called humor develops incorrect attitudes and should likewise not find place in the healthy home. Jokes based on prejudices too often convey the stereotypes upon which prejudices are learned. Seemingly innocent jokes based on racial differences or handicaps (mental or physical) too often pass on an attitude—a bias which is unhealthy both for family members and for persons to whom the biases are applied. Children will come to good interpersonal humor among themselves—they don't need the barrier of pre-conceived biases, taught in the name of humor.

On the other hand, don't condemn or over-react to the natural fun which children have together, just because among adults it would seem in poor taste. "Oh darling, don't be so crude!" a shocked mother of a grade school daughter exclaimed not long ago. The child had simply told a fat boyfriend, "You look like a butter-dumpling."

He did look like a butter-dumpling, and because she looked like a string bean he retaliated by saying so, thus sending both into hysterics. This was healthy, hilarious, preteen humor, but it left the mother dismayed.

In your family, work toward that elusive form of togetherness—of being comfortable; a rapport which enables the family members to see humor in the same situations, including family problems and your reactions to them. Work toward *refined* humor, gentle humor, as distinguished from the crude, slangy or rough versions, or the kind that depends on profanity or sexiness for its kicks. Dirty stories of any

kind are ruled out completely. Telling them anytime, any-
where, will soon blight a family fellowship beyond curing.
Building this personal and family programing is especially
mandatory if you expect to rear children who are emotion-
ally healthy and happy.

If this book helps you and your family to have some fun
together—if it helps you recall with delight your own family
background—if it helps you to see again the necessity of
humor—if it aids in developing your sensitivity to the humorous in your own family—we shall have succeeded in reaching
our goal.

Accidents

Eleven-year-old Ned Preston rushed into Hightower's Drug Store. "Quick!" he ordered. "My daddy is hanging by his trouser's leg from the top of our roof, his head down."

"Good heavens!" exclaimed the druggist. "Shall I . . . ?"

"Please put a new roll of film in my camera, quick!"

+

"Son," growled father, "how dare you kick your little brother in the stomach?"

"It's his own fault, Daddy. He turned around."

+

One housewife had an accident right near home. Afterward she called hubby on the phone and said, "Darling, I hate that neighbor you can't tolerate. He deliberately let me back my car right into his."

1

Mrs. Bill Norris drove her cute little Volkswagen into the garage and the mechanic came to greet her. "Now what would be your trouble, ma'am?" he asked politely.

"Well, it keeps having accidents," Mrs. Norris explained. "I don't know exactly why, but Bill says the trouble will stop if I'll just buy a new head for the driver. How much will a new one cost?"

+

The good lady was filling out an accident report blank, and she wrote as follows: "I had to back out of the driveway, and by the time I had backed out far enough to see what was coming, it already had."

+

Papa the fall guy is likely to fall literally. This one was being examined by the family doctor. "How come you have 309-741 tattooed on your back?" asked the doctor.

"That's not a tattoo mark," said papa, groaning. "That's where mama hit me with the car while I was holding the garage door open."

+

Drive like the wind today and you'll be gone with the wind tomorrow.

Adam

"Now, now, sweetheart," Adam purred, *"you can't possibly be jealous. You* know *I'm the first man on earth, and you're the first woman. We are the only two. There's nothing to be jealous of. Now is there, hm-m-m-m?"*

She smiled weakly then said, "I guess not. And still. . . ." She stopped, staring off at nothing.

He went on to sleep. She pretended to, but sometime after a while she lifted the bear skin off herself, went quietly to Adam's bed and very carefully counted his ribs!

+

In all of history there has been only one indispensable man — Adam.

+

Psychologists have decided positively why Adam was created before Eve. It was to give men one opportunity on earth to say something without being contradicted.

+

Plastics aren't new at all. How about Adam in the hands of Eve?

+

Adolescence

Here's a comforting thought for all us parents — adolescence, like snow, will gradually disappear if we ignore it long enough.

+

"Ashes to ashes, dust to dust," loftily sings one high schooler, "if radiation doesn't get you, psychiatry must."

+

Nothing disturbs a stern parent such as I like blowing his top in an impulsive moment of discipline, only to have his female teen-age victim smile sweetly and say, "Yes *indeedy,* father darling."

+

"The most irritating thing about the younger generation," says my neighbor, "is that I no longer belong to it."

+

Modern-day juveniles were a sorry lot, daddy felt; pampered, petted, spoiled. So he sounded off against his teen-age daughter. "Just look at your hair, for instance," he cried. "It looks like a mop."
Inquired she, innocently, "What's a mop?"

Adolescence is the age at which children stop asking questions and start questioning answers.

An adolescent is a person who is completely informed about anything he doesn't have to study.

+

When a wife begins to worry more about the fit of her shoes than the fit of her sweater, age is creeping up on her.

Adoption

"Shucks, I *know* I'm not adopted," declared one lad to another. "If I had been, they'd have sent me back before now."

Advice

They say a button on a man's coat is a sign that he belongs to Kiwanis, Rotary, Lions or some good lodge. A button *off* his coat is simply a sign that he is married.

+

If dad is coaching his big son about to enter business, he will say, "The Lord gave us two ends to use, Junior. One is to think with, the other to sit with. Our success depends on which we choose — and it's heads we win, tails we lose."

+

"Do you think women have a sense of humor?" Bill asked a friend. "Certainly. The more you humor them, the better they like it."

The salesman at the front door was giving a marvelous pitch. "This encyclopedia is priceless," he insisted. "It will tell you everything you need to know."

"Don't need one," said the harried husband, gently. "I'm married."

+

This story is told of the late Henry Ford, motor car manufacturer. At the Fords' golden wedding anniversary somebody asked Henry, "How do you account for your fifty years of happy married life?"

"My formula," the industrialist replied, "is the same as that I have always used in manufacturing automobiles — always stick to one model."

Age

Each of us "maturing" persons likes to hark back to his youth occasionally, and not a few of us try to regain it. Very few of us succeed, but one enviable old gent did. When aged about 80, he heard about some pills that would restore his youth, and naturally he wanted to try them. So he bought a box of 30. Then impatience seized him, so instead of taking one a day for 30 days, he swallowed all 30 in one big dose at bedtime. Next morning the family came in to wake him. They called and called, they shook and shook. Finally he turned over, yawned, opened one eye slowly, recognized his folks and said happily, "Okay, okay, I'll get up for breakfast, but I'm not going to school!"

"There's one thing about getting along in years," said one who was, *"you feel your corns worse than you feel your oats."*

+

Consider some of the compensations of age. 1.) You can hand the beautiful baby back to its mother, your daughter, when its diaper needs changing. 2.) You can call the younger generation's attention to all the mistakes it is making, without having to recognize any of your own.

+

Middle age is when all one's energy goes to waist.

+

When you become older, the rest of your days are likely to depend on the rest of your nights.

+

This was Uncle Hoot's 100th birthday, so of course the clan gathered to celebrate. He looked hale and hearty. Toward evening some friendly soul asked him, "Uncle Hoot, how have you managed to live so long and look so healthy?"

He explained willingly. "When I was twenty and married the missus, her and me made an agreement. We agreed that whenever we had any sort of an argument or unpleasantness, the loser would take a long walk so as to get over being mad."

"Yes," the listeners nodded. "Go on."

"Well, friends, I have benefited greatly these eighty years by exercise and fresh air."

If you are truly growing older, you need not worry much about avoiding temptation; along about now it just naturally starts avoiding you.

+

Middle age is when the young complain to you about the old and the old complain to you about the young.

+

The people hardest to convince they are of retirement age are not we ageing ones. They are our children at bedtime.

Agreements

"My husband and I both like the same things," said one lady recently. "Only it took him several years to learn."

+

"No, no, she should not accept the first man who asks her," ruled George Hall, talking with his Mary about their pretty young daughter. "If she wants to get married, let her wait until the right man comes along. Any other course would be a mistake."

"I know exactly what you mean," admitted Mary.

+

Economy-minded Mrs. Jones said, "Today I bought a girdle for the most astonishing figure."

Mr. Jones replied, "I understand. But how much did it cost?"

The officious neighbor lady disapproved of Mr. McTavish and his autocratic methods. "If I were your wife," said the busybody, a gal devoid of personality charm, "I'd give you poison."

Mr. McTavish bowed courteously and said, "And madam, if I were your husband, I'd take it."

Anniversaries

Sweetie Pie was bubbling. "Oh, Bill, darling, just think — it is nearly a year since we had that glorious honeymoon on the California beach, right there on the sand. Where will we spend our first anniversary?"

Replied Bill, realistically, "On the rocks."

+

Perhaps the cutest evidence of a money-minded husband came when a certain gentleman realized that today was his thirty-second wedding anniversary. He was out of town, so he telegraphed his wife $32 with this message: "Congratulations from your loving husband. And now would you like to try for $64?"

+

Housewife: "George, tomorrow's our twentieth wedding anniversary. I think I'll kill the big red rooster and bake him."

George: "Now, now, honey, why punish the poor chicken for what happened to me twenty years ago?"

*Mr. Doakes was a much harassed husband. He
tried to please her, heavens-to-betsy yes! But you
know how it goes sometimes.*

*Came their wedding anniversary and she gave
him two neckties, one blue and one red. He kissed
her, thanked her over and over. Still she said, "I
suppose you don't like the gift."*

*"But sweetheart I do!" he insisted. "Here, I'll
show you." He took off the old tie he was wearing,
and put the new blue one on right there. "See?" he
beamed. "I like it. Thank you very much."*

*She still looked glum. She sighed in her
self-martyrdom and said, "So you don't like red,
huh?"*

Appreciation

Maybe you heard about the Vermont farmer, a
relative of taciturn Calvin Coolidge. After forty
years of marriage, he ate a particularly fine supper
one night then turned to his wife and said, "Sylvia,
when I consider how much you have meant to me
all these years, sometimes it's terrible hard not to
tell you."

+

*Little Sonny walked six blocks over to his
Auntie's house and said, "Thank you very
much for the present you sent me."*

*"Oh," gushed pleased Auntie, "you should-
n't have done that. It didn't amount to
anything."*

*"Yes," Sonny agreed, "that's what I
thought, too. But Mother made me come
way over here to thank you anyway."*

Willie and his mother were sitting together on a train. A lady across the aisle smiled and gave Willie an orange. He took it, but remained silent.

"What do you say to the nice lady, Willie?" Mother prodded.

Said Willie, handing back the orange, "Peel it."

Ardor

The sorority girls were hearing a report from one of their sisters. "He kissed me four times in a row," said Rosie.

"Yes, yes, go on," the others chorused. "Then what?"

"Then he began to get sentimental."

+

"Oh, Willis, you are much too slow!" the girl cried.

"I don't quite grasp you," said the scholarly young man.

Cried she, "That's just it!"

+

He was standing closer. And closer. Then closer still. They were outside the chemistry building. Possibly some sort of spiritual osmosis was taking place — who knows? At any rate he murmured into her dainty shell-like ear, "Elaine, what would you say if I kissed you?"

Replied she, "I wouldn't be in a position to say anything."

He finally cornered her there in the library entry hall. "S-say, Susie," he began, "I g-guess you didn't know wh-who I was when I met you there by the stadium yesterday, d-did you?"

"No," admitted desperate Sue. "Who were you?"

+

"Am I the first girl you ever kissed?" asked luscious Lucille.

"Now that I think of it," said her gallant courtier, "you do look familiar."

+

The moon was trailing its golden beams through the willows and out onto the gently rippling waves of Valentine Bay. The sweet fragrance of honeysuckle filled the air. Nearby, a lone night bird called softly, melodiously, to its mate. The young man on the bench touched the young lady's hand and murmured, "Last night I dreamed I was married to the most beautiful girl in all the world."

Said she, "And were we happy?"

+

"Oh, my darling," he panted, "if you refuse me, I shall die."

Well, sad to relate, she did refuse him. And 61 years later, he died.

+

"If you refuse to marry me," declared the ardent senior, "I will blow my brains out."

"What a joke that will be on father," said Sue. "He doesn't think you have any."

Arguments

Why do red-headed women always marry quiet men? They don't. The poor fellows just get that way afterward.

+

"Tell me, mister," said the young housewife, hands on hips, chin out, "did somebody tell you how wonderful you are?"

Vanity touched, he replied, "Why no, I don't think so."

"Then where did you get the idea?"

+

Often a husband's words have to be very pointed, in order to get them in edgewise.

+

"You stay quiet," a big-bosomed matron ordered her pipsqueak husband at the party. "When I want your opinion, I'll give it to you."

+

Buck and Lucy were having quite a spat. They had reached the stage of strained silence, and it lasted for twenty minutes as they rolled down the highway. Presently they turned a curve and saw a donkey by the roadside. As they got closer, the animal brayed. Lucy waved to it.

"Relative of yours, I assume," said Buck, grimly.

"Yes," Lucy admitted. "By marriage."

"Ed and I have been married for seven years," said Virginia, "and we've never had a quarrel. Oh, sometimes there's a difference of opinion; but when I'm right, Ed immediately gives in."

"How nice," their pastor agreed, listening politely. "And what if Ed is right?"

"That's never happened."

+

They were going at it hammer and tongs. "Women are nuts," he raved. "Why, for instance, do you go to the movies and cry over the antics of some silly actors you've never even met?"

"For the same reason that you men go to a ball game, then stand up and yell for a man you never met just because he's safe at second base."

+

The proud papa was studying his offspring. "He's very smart," said papa. "He gets his intelligence from me."

"He must," wifey agreed. "I've still got mine."

+

Papa was the type who runs off at the mouth and needs to be hushed up frequently. He was in good form this morning. "I am a self-made man," he declared at the breakfast table.

Mama sighed and murmured, "Well! I'm glad to know it. You have just relieved the Lord of a terrific responsibility."

Babies

Storks often work disguised as physicians. Five-year-old Johnny was not too pleased with the looks of his new baby sister, but he refrained from comment at first. Then one day the doctor called to make a routine check on the baby, and happened to bring his own little girl along. She was a doll, charming, beautiful. Johnny looked at the visiting girl then at his homely little sister, and said to his mother, "Boy! the doctor sure picks the best ones for himself."

+

The young father had been pacing the hospital corridor for hours and hours. Finally the beaming nurse came out of the delivery room with a large bundle of blankets. Newpapa rushed up to her and demanded, "Hurry, tell me! Is it a boy?"

She smiled sweetly at him and replied, "Well, the one in the middle is."

+

Little Miss Harriet was showing off her baby sister to a friend. "Who brought her?" asked the friend.

"Dr. Grady."

"Oh, fine, we take from him too."

+

Have you heard about the baby ear of corn? He asked, "Mama, where did I come from?"

And Mama Corn replied, "Hush, darling, the stalk brought you."

One bachelor was a distinguished attorney with a lawyer's passion for language that meant exactly what he said and said exactly what he meant. So when he viewed his sister's new baby, he reported on it downtown at his club as follows: "Yes, a fine baby boy. Very red of countenance, clean shaven, small features, and a constant drinker."

+

Calvin Detwiler was holding his husky son Jerry Franklin one day. Presently he turned to his pretty wife Florence and said, "Hey, isn't it about time this lad learned to say 'Daddy'?"

"No, no, dear, not yet," she hastened to say. "I hoped we wouldn't have to tell him who you are until he got a little older."

+

Your baby is the sweetest, most beautiful one ever born? How odd that we should meet! So is mine.

+

The scene here is at the hospital. Nurse is holding the new baby up to the big plate glass window. New papa is outside looking in, and is making all manner of grotesque faces, waggling his fingers on his ears, and generally acting dumb, being under the delusion that this is the way to amuse little-people-in-arms. But the wise nurse comforts baby by crooning, "Don't you feel ashamed, sweetheart. All fathers act goofy like that for the first few days."

In the second grade at school the teacher was working on vocabulary. She was trying to explain what the word "collision" means. "A collision," she said, "is usually very noisy. It's when two things come together unexpectedly. Now who can give an example?"

Shouted one lad, "Twins!"

+

It was that same father who, at the birth of his fourth, was a little nonchalant about it. When he saw the nurse approach him from the delivery room, he arose and asked, "Well, nurse, will this one be using a razor or lipstick?"

+

Very young Barry Richard Naylor, my little neighbor, proudly told his school teacher the good news at home. "We've got a new little brother named Robert Paul and you have to come to see him, ma'am."

"Thanks, Barry," said his teacher. "But perhaps I'd better wait until your mother has fully recovered."

"You don't need to be scared," Barry reassured her. "It ain't catching."

+

When you see a mother in action you can always tell whether it's the first baby or the fifth. If it's the first, she'll be carrying it like a rare old heirloom vase. If it's the fifth, like a ragged old raincoat.

Most times the nursery should be given a Brooklynese pronunciation — "noisery."

+

From six to sixteen months babies strain to learn to talk. When they're sixteen months to sixteen years, they face parents straining to keep them quiet.

+

"I wish she'd been a boy," said the small big brother of his new sister, "then he could have played football and gone fishing with me."

"Well, why not exchange her for a brother?" asked the friend.

"Can't. We've already used her for nearly a week."

+

Two men were walking down the street. One looked up then said, "Look out, there comes Jack Glenn. He's got a new baby and he'll talk our ears off."

"No, take it easy," said the second man. "Right behind him I see Bud Hale coming, and he's just back from a successful fishing trip. All we have to do is introduce them and let nature take its course."

+

"Baby may be the king in your home," one harried husband said to another, "but in ours he's the prince of wails."

"Hey, honey," Mr. Youngfather called to his wife from his desk in the den, "I'm writing out the checks. Two more payments and the baby is ours!"

+

The father was proudly showing off his young son in the living room. "Yes, sir, he's been walking like that now for ten months."

"Astounding!" murmured the friend, a bachelor. "Is there no way at all to make him sit down?"

Bachelors

Conceit is indeed many splendored. "I have a profound admiration for girls," said one young bachelor to his date. "I think they are very beautiful. But I would never think of marrying one of them. No, sir, never!"

"Indeed," murmured his companion. "You not only admire girls, but you have a sincere consideration for their welfare."

+

One bachelor finally got engaged to a sweet girl, but she soon discovered his real personality and returned all his letters marked "Fourth Class Male."

+

Don't get the idea that no bachelor can understand women. What do you think makes a man a bachelor?

Pretty Linda Foster, a University of Arizona co-ed, on the sorority house porch was straining to be courteous. Her caller spoke — "Ah, Linda, I've never seen such dreamy eyes before."

She lost control. "You've never stayed this late before."

+

Handsome young Thomas had never gotten married, and one day a pal asked him why. "Because," explained Tom, "I have never yet met a girl who already owns a mink coat and has already had her tonsils and appendix removed."

+

Ask any young unmarried man — few things in this world are more expensive than a pretty girl who is free for the evening.

+

The bachelor guest had been in the Reynolds home for two hours, and was entranced by the freedom allowed the small son, Kip. The lad was pounding nails into the tables, the chairs, the TV set, even the piano, and the parents seemed not to mind.

"Uh, isn't that a rather expensive method of play your little boy has?" the guest asked Mr. Reynolds. "How can you afford it?"

"Not very expensive," the fond father replied. "You see, I get the nails whole-sale."

A car skidded, hit a power pole, turned over and came down so as to pin John underneath. He wasn't badly hurt but he couldn't be removed very easily. While they waited for a wrecker, the policeman in charge got out his notebook and began to question him.

"Name, sir?"

"John P. Smith."

"Married?"

"No, officer, this is the worst fix I was ever in."

+

"Daddy," questioned little son — "what is a bachelor?"

"It's a man who didn't have a car when he was young."

Banking

Uncle Sebe Jones couldn't write, so the bank just let him sign his checks like this: X X.

After a year or so, the checks began to come in signed X X X. One day his banker friend saw him and asked how come.

"Well sir, we struck oil on our land," Sebe explained, "and I don't have to farm no more. And my Miranda, well she figured now we could be in sassiety and I ought to have a middle name."

Bathrooms

The old wooden privy had done service for years. Then one day father stormed into the house, called his small but gangly son, and demanded to know who had pushed the privy over backward into the creek.

"I did, Father," the lad admitted, demurely.

"Come with me," Pop ordered. "I'll whale the daylights out of you."

"But Father," the boy protested while being led by the ear, "remember George Washington. His father did not punish him when he told the truth."

"I know all about that," Pop growled. "I also know that George Washington's father wasn't sitting in the cherry tree."

Birthdays

The birthday party had sort of gotten out of hand. In desperation the mother clapped her hands for attention then announced: "And there will be a very special prize for the first child who goes home."

+

Another birthday party was going fine, and little Toria (short for Victoria) was enjoying herself. The honoree's mother approached and said, "Toria darling, will you have another helping of ice cream?"

"My mother told me not to," the little girl admitted. "But when she did that, I don't think she realized how tiny the helpings would be."

Young Mollie Mallory needed divine guidance and — as we all should — asked for it: "Dear God, please help me save my dimes to buy daddy a birthday present. And be sure not to let the ice cream wagon come down our street for a while."

+

Willie and Tommy had been disagreeing — call it that — for several days, sometimes to the point of violence. Then came the time for Willie to send invitations to his birthday party. Mother demanded that he send one to Tommy. Willie demurred, but under pressure finally agreed to invite his bosom enemy.

The day came. All the other kids arrived for the party, but not Tommy. "Did you invite him as I told you?" Mother asked.

"Sure I did, Mommy," Willie declared. "I not only invited him to come, I *dared* him to."

Boyfriends

She was brushing him off. He'd been hanging around too much, and a handsomer lad was courting her now anyway. But he fought back — "I'll have you know I'm nobody's fool!"

"Cheer up, laddie," the girl said, loftily. "Maybe some kind soul will adopt you."

Another girl was trying to brush her friend off, too. They met on the high school campus.

"Whatsa idea giving me such a dirty look?" he snarled.

"You've got a dirty look, sure enough," said she, "but I didn't give it to you."

+

The irate father came to the head of the stairs, blood in his eye. "Hey, you down there!" he shouted to the lad courting his daughter. "It's nearly 3 a.m. Do you think you can stay all night?"

"Thank you, sir," answered the hero, in surprise. "But I'd have to phone my mother first."

+

Young lady, to her friend: "Daddy is very pleased to know you are a poet, Crumley."

Crumley: "Is he? Why?"

Young lady: "Well, the last time he tried to throw out one of my boy friends, it happened to be a professional wrestler."

+

"What did Chuck mean when he said you looked ethereal?" Joan asked pretty Gail, a sophomore.

"I didn't know," Gail admitted, "so I slapped him anyway, just to be on the safe side."

Boys

Mother, father and little Sonny drove up to renowned "Sky Y" Camp in the beautiful mountains. Presently the parents were talking to the husky he-man camp director. "Our Horatio usually has his tantrum about 3 o'clock in the afternoon," said mother. "Will any of the camp activities interfere with that schedule?"

+

"Horrors, Bobby!" mother exclaimed. "Just look at you! Face dirty and scratched, clothes muddy, one shoe off. How many times have I told you never to play with that bad Smith boy?"

Bobby looked up at her, aggrieved. "Do I look like I have been playing?"

+

"Shouldn't you take little Albert to the zoo this morning?" mother suggested one Saturday.

"Heavens, no," said long-suffering daddy. "If the zoo wants him, let them come and get him."

+

Pressure on the mother and her three-year-old son was such that they were pushed away back in the elevator. "Aren't you afraid he'll be mashed?" a solicitous stranger asked.

"Not I," mother smiled. "He bites!"

Mrs. Betty Smith sent her small son Stevie over to the seed store, and Ed McDonald the proprietor welcomed him. "Mother wants a bottle of spray," said Stevie, "that will kill weeds and cutworms and crab grass and beetles. And spinach."

Brothers

Mother had a splitting headache. So she ordered big brother to take little brother out while she tried to sleep. "Give him anything he wants to keep him quiet," she ordered. "Do whatever he says."

Peace reigned for a half hour, then little brother began yelling. "Whatever is wrong now?" demanded mother at the window.

"Well," reported big brother, "he wanted me to dig a big hole in the ground for him, and I did. But now he wants me to bring it into the living room."

+

"Where is your sister, Bobbie?" the pastor asked, as he called.

"She's in the house practicing our piano duet. I beat her done."

+

Johnny: "Mother, you have given brother a much bigger helping of pie than you gave me."

Mother: "But sweetheart, brother is a much bigger boy than you are."

Johnny: "Well, shucks, he always will be, if this keeps up."

*"Who started this fight?" the indig-
nant mother demanded of the boys.
"Well," explained Bobbie, "it really
began when Joey hit me back."*

+

People were always telling nine-year-old Daisy
Mae what a big girl she was, and it didn't sit well
with four-year-old Burtie. *He* felt big too. One day,
walking toward church, Burtie asked his mama,
"How old would you say I look?"

She understood, so she replied tactfully, "Oh,
I'd say about eight."

"Boy, mommie," the lad beamed. "You know
something? You look to be about a hundred!"

+

*Two small boys rushed into Dr. Herbert Wes-
sell's dental office. "I need a tooth pulled quick,
Doc," said one. "And don't use gas, cause I'm in a
hurry."*

*"How brave you are," said Doc. "Which tooth is
it?"*

*The lad turned to his smaller companion and
ordered, "Git up in the chair and show him which
tooth aches, brother."*

Budgets

*The man and his missus sat at their desk before a
stackup of bills, some of them months old. Both
looked glum. Then she came up with a sensible
solution to their problem, saying, "The only fair
course to take is to flip a coin — heads I spend less,
tails you earn more."*

"It's almost impossible to keep the household accounts straight," lamented Mrs. Hazeburch to her neighbor. "Already this month I've had to write in six mistakes, in order to make our books balance properly."

+

Mama had been sitting at her desk wrestling with the family budget, and papa sat with the kids nearby. Presently she turned to them and reported, "Well, I have a budget set up for the family, but one of us will have to go."

+

Young Mr. Jerry Detwiler, married only a few months, knew that his wife Rosie needed a vacuum cleaner, so they agreed to buy one. When he came home from work the next day, he was distressed to see that instead of the simpler model, she had bought the shiny, chromium-fitted deluxe.

"But sweetie," she explained logically, "this fancy one won't cost any more. All we have to do is pay on it a few additional months."

Burglars

This scene is the living room at 3 a.m. A burglar has entered the home. Daddy, trembling but brave, hears the burglar, gropes around, finds Junior's water pistol and faces the outlaw with it. The burglar is scared, too, and stands hands high, waiting for the police to come.

At that moment, in comes little Junior clad in pajamas and says, "Go on, Daddy, squirt him with it."

Cars

The family was on vacation in their big Cadillac, but trouble developed so they limped into the nearest garage. The mechanic studied the sad looking condition of the car, then asked the owner, "Whatever happened to you, sir?"

"We were hit by one of those little Volkswagens."

"Goodness, how many times?"

+

Little Willie was merely asking his mother a sensible question, wanting as all children do to get information. "Mother, what becomes of an automobile when it gets too old to run?"

She answered, "Some smart salesman pawns it off on your father."

+

Any motorist can tell you that the hardest noise in the world to ignore is a squeak in a new car.

+

The young-married Jerry Detwilers bought their first new car, and naturally wanted to be economical with it. So they listened to every salesman who happened into town. After a while Rosie Detwiler wrote her mother: "We bought a timer that saved 30 percent of the gas, new spark plugs that saved 40 percent, a fancy new carburetor that saved another 40 percent. And so after we had driven about 20 miles, our gas tank overflowed."

The wary tourist stopped at a garage in an eastern town and began to look around. Presently he approached the service manager and said, "Your place seems to be run very efficiently, so I want some work done on my car. I like efficiency. I was just noticing that mechanic yonder. Before he went to work on that Thunderbird, he washed his hands, spread a cloth so as not to smudge anything, raised and lowered the hood gently, generally showed a love for the vehicle."

"Yep," said the man. "That's his own car."

+

Two sisters were on vacation in their car, which was new. After the first hundred miles or so they pulled into a garage and said to the mechanic, "Something must be wrong with our car. It keeps hitting things."

+

Some cars, even these modern ones, use much more gas than we'd like them to. The Jukes family, however, owned a prehistoric crate which drank the stuff. One day they all piled into it and started on vacation. Fifty miles from home they pulled up at a filling station; all got out and rushed to the rest rooms except papa, who stayed there with his motor running. "Fill her up," he ordered.

The attendant began to pump in gasoline. He pumped and pumped and pumped. Presently he peered carefully into the man's tank then said, "Would you mind turning the motor off? You are gaining on me."

Checks

Jim Jones the salesman, actually a very loyal husband and father, was away from home and sent his pretty wife Jane a gift check. Instead of money, though, he had filled in the amount space thus: "One million kisses."

No mean kidder herself, Mrs. Jones telegraphed him at his next stop: "Thanks for the check. The milkman cashed it."

Children

One six-year-old cutie-pie who had been naughty was duly scolded by both parents. At supper, immediately after the hassle, a contrite papa and mama asked little Betsy if she would like to return thanks. She would. She bowed her sweet curly head and murmured, "I thank thee, Lord, that thou hast prepared a table for me in the presence of mine enemies."

+

Young P. B. and Stevie Smith, my astute neighbors, went into the lawn-mowing business. On the third Saturday morning, they started out slowly, and rather late. "Shouldn't you hurry if you want to get a lot of jobs?" mother asked.

"Oh, no," they reported from the depths of experience. "We don't dare apply too early. We get most of our jobs from men who have already mowed about half of their lawns."

Mother: "I want us to get Junior a bicycle for Christmas."

Father: "Maybe we should. Do you think it will help keep him from being so unruly and mean?"

Mother: "No. But at least it will spread his meanness over more territory."

+

Exasperated Pop: "When Abraham Lincoln was your age, he worked hard all day and studied his books hard at night."

Growing Son: "Yes, and when he was your age, he was President."

Clubs

Mrs. McSnoot was really snooting the other girls at the bridge party. "I'd like to remind all of you," said she, in an attempt at airiness, "that in terms of ancestry you are nobody. Nobody at all. But *my* family landed at Plymouth Rock."

"And you," one lady snapped back, "I presume, crawled out from under it."

+

Vain Mrs. Noxious was showing her photo album to the girls at club meeting. One lady soon had enough of it. Presently Mrs. Noxious showed a portrait of herself as a little girl sitting on her mother's lap, and remarked, "This is how I looked 17 years ago."

"Really?" breathed the fed up lady. "And who is the child you are holding?"

"My husband is such a child, the way I have to look after him," rattled Mrs. Wilson at club meeting. *"I don't know what would happen to him if I had to be gone for a week or two. Why, when he's sewing on buttons, darning his socks or mending anything, I even have to thread the needle for him."*

+

"Is Mrs. Anderson an active member of your sewing circle?" somebody asked Mrs. Jones.
"Goodness, no. She never says a word. Just sits there and sews."

College

But don't you good people get the idea that *every*body ought to go in for higher education? No sir, not at all. Some of you young people have got to go right to work, in order to work up so you can hire the college graduates we are turning out.

+

"My son in college writes that he is a great athlete," said fond mother. "He's burning up the track, he says."
"Wouldn't doubt it," a friend agreed. "I visited the athletic field last week, and when I saw the track it had nothing but cinders on it."

*Letter from college son to father: NO
MON. NO FUN. YOUR SON.*
*Letter from father to college son:
TOO BAD. HOW SAD. YOUR DAD.*

+

*The letter had just come from son at college.
"Did he pass all his examinations?" dad demanded
of mother.*
*"Well, no, dear. But he's only fourth from the
top of those who failed."*

Confidences

One night daughter came in from a date and
exclaimed to mother, "Oh I just know Wilbur is
the man for me, Momsie! Every time he holds me
close, I can hear his heart pounding."

"Now, now," soothed Mom, "just be careful.
For nearly a year your father fooled me that way
by wearing a dollar watch."

+

*Melissa was gabbling to Mom about
her social affairs. "I wonder if you aren't
getting George and Horace confused,"
said Mom.*
*"I sure am!" Daughter giggled. "I
confuse George one night and Horace
the next!"*

"Now, young lady," Mom demanded at 3 a.m., "why are you so late getting in?"

"Oh. We were out driving, and Johnnie lost his bearings."

"My, my!" murmured Mom. "In my day the young men ran out of gas."

Dating

Self-conscious girl on date, "Is my face dirty, or is it my imagination?"

"I don't know about your imagination," said her boy friend, "but your face looks clean."

+

"Why do you date Oswald?" one teenager asked her friend. "He can't dance."

"No," the friend admitted, "but he sure can intermission."

+

Daughter's caller looked a little dangerous, so Father met him when he arrived and said, "We turn out the lights in this house at 10:30."

Said the boy, "Thanks, that's nice of you, sir."

+

Another father said the same thing — "We turn out the lights in this house at 10:30."

Said this boy: "That's all right, sir. Gloria and I won't be reading."

Son, about to go out for the evening, to father who was lecture minded: "Yes, sir, certainly I know the value of a dollar. That's why I asked for five."

+

"I wish I could be like the Army," wailed teen-age Jeannie, "and always have a reserve manpower pool."

Daughters

I bought me a new summer suit in conservative salt-and-pepper gray. "Take it back," my daughters ordered. "Get beige trousers, a tan sports jacket and a sea-green necktie. What are you trying to do, look your age?"

+

One daughter came in beaming because beach lifeguards voted her the girl they'd most like to rescue. So Mom dug out her scrapbook showing that in 1923 oil drillers in Houston, Texas, chose her as the girl they'd most like to gush over.

+

Our ten-year-old Babe is now socially adjusted again. She discovered that the way to handle that tough, overbearing, twelve-year-old new boy in the neighborhood was simply to sock him once under the chin and twice in the belly. Now he's a loyal lieutenant in her gang.

Our married daughter Judy is a young woman of great perspicacity. "In case you are throwing anything away during housecleaning, mother," said she, airily, while visiting us Saturday morning, "remember Pat and I are furnishing our new home." It netted her half a truck load of loot.

+

My high school daughter tripped in singing late yesterday, gave me a kiss, and told me what a grand pops I am. But I have narrowed it down; she either wants the car Saturday night, or a new formal. Or both.

Decisions

"Mother, when I grow up will I have a husband just like Daddy?"

"Why of course, honey."

Silence for a few moments. Then — "And if I never get married, will I be an old maid like Miss Weems?"

"Yes, of course."

More silence for meditation, then a murmur — "Creepers, a girl certainly is faced with a dim future, isn't she?"

+

Mother the food wrangler gave her small daughter 50 cents then asked what she proposed to buy with it.

"Well, I'll get me some candy and some ice cream and some peanuts and some popcorn and —" here she looked up and saw the dark look on mother's face — "and a nice green vegetable with vitamins in it."

Definitions

Mr. J. Franklin Detwiler had a habit of calling his wife "angel," and a friend asked him why. "Because," said J. F., "she never has an earthly thing to wear, she's always harping on something, and is always ready to fly."

+

Did you folks hear about the happy cave man? He gave his wife thumping to remember him by.

Dialogue

The Grays had company. Mr. Gray was in fine fettle and kept springing clever jokes, wisecracks, epigrams. Presently one of the men turned to little Judy Gray and said, "My, my, sweetheart, but your daddy is very funny, isn't he?"

"I guess so," said she. "Anyhow when we have company."

+

Little Dixie Dee, having moved into the neighborhood just the day before, took some of her brothers and sisters across the hedge to visit. "My, my, how many children are in your family?" the neighbor man asked.

"Nine," said D.D.

"They must cost a lot."

"We don't buy 'em," said D.D. "We raise 'em."

"What is a monologue, Daddy?" little son asked.

"That's a conversation between a man and a wife."

"Teacher said that was a dialogue."

"Your teacher isn't married, son."

+

Roseann had reached the mature age of five. She was perched on a box in Daddy's workshop watching him make things, and was, of course, peppering him with questions, and answering many of them herself. Daddy was trying to concentrate on a knotty problem in carpentry. "Hey, be quiet, can't you?" he pleaded.

"No," she ruled wisely. "I'm going to keep on talking. I don't have to keep quiet. I'm a woman."

+

"For heaven's sake, stop asking so many questions, Margaret," cried mother. "Curiosity killed the cat."

After two minutes of meditation, little Maggie asked, "What did the cat want to know?"

Diets

A group of ladies were calling at Mrs. Ned Preston's home. Little Eugenia Preston of course barged in. "My, my, Eugenia," said one, "you surely are growing. And what will you do when you get to be as big as your mother?"

Said Eugenia: "Diet."

Professor Robert J. Hannelly, Ph.D., head man of Phoenix College and a distinguished scholar, was at home one evening reading *The National Geographic Magazine.* His sweet wife Gene was knitting nearby. They had lived much, and the marks of the good, well-fed years were upon them. Dr. Hannelly, thumbing his magazine, came to an article with photos on southern Europe, and presently he remarked, casually, "I wonder if you have any idea what makes the Tower of Pisa lean?"

His Gene shifted gently in her chair and shook her head. "No. If I did, I'd take some myself."

+

And to many wives — ah, me — reducing is nothing more than wishful shrinking.

+

An adipose neighbor settled into one of Reg Manning's patio chairs to discuss his troubles. "I have to watch my waistline every minute," sighed the fat man.

"Mighty fortunate, then," suggested Reg, "that you have it right out there in front of you where you can."

Discipline

Papa had gotten tough. He was washing the dinner dishes, and he had stood his very young son on a chair to do the drying. But the son protested: "Why do I have to help? *You* married her."

The two little human roosters had made it clear that they held no love for one another. Finally one said he was ready to fight. The other demurred.

"You're just afraid of me, that's all," said the first.

"No such thing. But if I fought, mother would find out and give me a hard whipping."

"She can't see us here. How'd she find out?"

"She'd see the doctor going into your house."

+

"Where'd you get that bloody cut on the side of your head?" Pop demanded of his son. "Who gave it to you?"

"Nobody, sir."

"Nobody? Think carefully what you are saying. Nobody?"

"No sir, nobody gave it to me. I got it in exchange for a black eye, a sprained arm and a bloody nose."

+

"Does your mother spank you?" Little Jeannie asked Bobby.

"Yes."

"Does your daddy spank you?"

"Yes."

"Who hurts the most?"

"I do."

Divorce

It's possible that a harem would be harder to handle than a wife. But did you ever hear of a divorced harem?

*John Profyle, the handsome motion picture star,
was pouring out his love to a prospective seventh
wife. She was reluctant to give him her answer.*

*"Maybe I shouldn't marry you, John," said she.
"I've heard some shocking things the other girls
said about you."*

*"Ignore them," he purred. "They're just old
wives' tales."*

+

The farm couple had been quarreling. They'd
spat and sass and say unkind things. Then one day,
driving to town together, they passed a lake with
some waterfowl on it. "Just look yonder at that
goose and gander," said Ma. "Gliding along together nice and peaceful, loving one another.
Wouldn't it be nice if people could be that way?"

Pa never answered, just stared straight ahead.

Come late afternoon, the two were returning,
and again they saw a goose and gander on the lake.
So Ma spoke up again: "Just look at that goose and
gander, Pa. So peaceful. Wouldn't it be nice if we
could live like that?"

"Ef you'll take a closer look, Ma," said Pa,
sullenly, "you'll notice that there ain't the same
gander."

+

The back-country husband came to the doctor's
office with his head all banged up. "Been in a
terrible fight, I see," said the Doc, swabbing
wounds. "Sam, why don't you stay out of bad
company?"

"Doc," said poor Sam, "I'd shore do it, but I
just can't find enough money to pay for a
divorce."

The movie actress was telling her little
girl a bedtime story — very accurately,
too. She began: "Once upon a time there
was a mama bear, a papa bear, and a
baby bear by a previous marriage."

+

Two little kids so unfortunate as to be children
of Hollywood's less admirable set were talking.
Said the first boy, "My daddy can lick your
daddy."

"Are you crazy?" demanded the second. "Your
daddy *is* my daddy!"

Driving

Coffee nerves? Heavens to betsy, policemen get
them whenever our wives drive. A motorcycle cop
saw one of the sweet things weaving up a street.
She seemed to be alone in her car, yet she kept
looking down, and her car wobbled from curb to
curb. He whizzed up to her, and when she stopped
he saluted and said, "You seemed to be in trouble,
ma'am. Were you feeling faint or something?"

"Dear me no, officer," she gave him her nicest
smile. "I'm quite all right. I was just looking at this
book of wallpaper samples."

+

Two ladies — call them that — drove
their cars toward each other on a little
narrow street. Neither could pass. One
lady leaned out and shrieked, "I never
back up for a stupid idiot!"

"I always do!" shouted the other,
shifting into reverse.

They were breezing down the highway. "Stop *going so fast, Jim,"* the Mrs. *ordered.*

"Why?" *he snarled.*

"Because there's a policeman on a motorcycle behind us and he can't get by with you going so fast."

+

The motorcycle cop flagged papa over to the curb, came and leaned on the door and began his sarcastic routine. But mama in the back seat took over at once. "You are quite right, officer. He *was* going fast. He's always doing something. He's a reckless, inconsiderate, selfish male. All the time I try to tell him how to conduct himself, but he just goes right ahead and ignores me and acts like a contemptible—"

The cop, himself married, pulled away, saluted the man at the wheel and said, "Drive on, friend."

+

Henry Smith unfortunately drove his car into a post. The cop who rushed up asked why he had lost control.

"My exasperator is to blame for it," said Henry.

"I guess you mean your accelerator," suggested the officer.

"No, I mean what I said."

"Well for pete's sake, what part of a car is the exasperator?"

"There she sits, officer, in the back seat."

+

No housewife really has any trouble parking the family car. It's just that, after having parked, she is never quite sure which of three meters to put the nickel in.

Economy

My dear wife gets a little hazy at times. Once she got us on an economy spree. Come the week end, and she chewed me out. Said she, "Monday you liked beans, Tuesday you liked beans, Wednesday you liked beans, Thursday you liked beans. Now how come suddenly on Friday you don't like beans?"

+

Two Scotsmen were at the club, and one kept jingling something in a coat pocket. Finally the other inquired if he was playing with coins.

"No," Sandy replied. "I am holding my wife's teeth. There has been too much eating between meals in our home."

+

The young couple had to economize, so she tried every conceivable way to cook inexpensive hamburger attractively. After a while the husband began asking each night at the table, "How now, ground cow?"

Engagements

A salesman rang the door bell. Little Sylvia answered. "Is your mother engaged?" asked the man.

"She's already married," said Sylvia.

Extravagance

"Hey, we can't afford to run four electric fans all day," the husband scolded his wife. "You are being too extravagant."

"No such thing," she shot back. "They aren't costing us a cent. I borrowed them from the vacant apartment next door."

Failure

Papa was lecturing. "Nothing, no nothing, is impossible to accomplish if you really try," orated he.

Said little sonny: "Let me see you push toothpaste back into the tube."

Faithfulness

Rosie, shortly after marriage: "Oh, you men are all alike. You went to that show last night just to look at the pretty girls."

Jerry, very honest: "That's not true, darling. Pretty girls never interest me. It's you I love."

+

"All men are fools," declared the wife.

"Of course, dear," he agreed. "We are made like that so you girls won't have to be old maids."

+

When you see a man bringing flowers to his wife for no reason — there's a reason.

Fights

The Smiths went to a party at long last, their first one in a long, long time. John, unfortunately acted up, overdid himself. When they got back home Mrs. Smith tied into him. After chewing him out for 15 minutes or so, she concluded with: "If this were just the first time, I could overlook it, John. But you embarrassed me the same way in January of 1960."

+

"Women are inconsistent," lamented Joesephus Doakes to a friend. "Mine chased me out of the house with a rolling pin this morning. Then she cried because I neglected to kiss her good-bye."

+

Mrs. Doakes went around the house frowning at her husband for two days over some fancied slight. He was sorry for it, but he couldn't get her to loosen up. Then on the second night she suddenly let go and smiled beautifully.

"Hey, darling," said he, "does that mean I am forgiven?"

"Not at all," she snarled. "I'm just resting my face."

+

The reporter was interviewing a former circus man. "And so you were married in a cage of wild tigers, sir?"

"Yes, that's right."

"Didn't it seem mighty exciting?"

"It did then. It wouldn't now."

Any husband is sure to tremble when his wife eyes him straight-on and says, "I want to talk to you."

+

If a man gives in when he's wrong, he is a wise man. If he gives in when he is right, he is married.

+

Men struck by lightning each year outnumber women six to one. And there's an equally scientific reason — the lightning doesn't want to get struck back at!

+

In San Francisco a native was describing their most recent real estate adjustment (earthquake).
"I saw the chandelier swinging," said he. "Then bricks began to fall. And then cups and saucers started flying all over the dining room."
"Heavens, that reminds me!" muttered one listener. "I forgot to mail some letters my wife gave me."

+

Sympathy cards should be sent to this gentleman, married to a waspish rib. "I dreamed," said he, "that my wife and a beautiful movie star were fighting over me, and my wife was winning."

+

One Mr. and Mrs. had been arguing violently for hours. Finally he had enough of it, so he said, "Sweetheart, I have been thinking, and I have decided that I agree with you."

"You're too late," she snapped. "It won't do you any good. I've changed *my* mind."

The prosecuting attorney was excited. Even Judge Jennings leaned over the desk, eagerly listening. "Why, *why,* madam," said the attorney dramatically, eyes gleaming, arm waving, "*why* did you shoot your husband with a bow and arrow? Oh *why?*"

She looked innocently at them and at the jury, then replied, "Because I didn't want to wake the children."

Finances

It's 2 or 3 a.m. and the Mrs. hears a noise. "HsssT, Tom, wake up!" she whispers to her husband, shaking him gently. "I'm sure a burglar is going through your pockets."

Says Tom, "Well, you two will just have to fight it out between you."

+

A neighbor man ambled over and said, "Did you give your wife that lecture on economy we talked about?"

"Yep."

"And with what results?"

"I'm to give up golf, beer and cigarettes."

+

The husband in this instance finally won a few extra dollars on the races, so he gave it all to his wife, saying, "Go buy yourself some decent clothes, honey."

Replied Honey, "I won't do it. All my life I've been wearing decent clothes. Now I'm going to dress like other women."

Hubby was fed up. He'd paid for this and paid for that until he was near the breaking point. But now in came the little woman with yet a new proof of extravagance — a silly effort at millinery which looked like a piece of radar equipment, and would cost about the same. "Where in the world do you think I'm going to get the money to pay for it?" he thundered.

And she replied sweetly, "Honey man, you know I'm not inquisitive."

+

Two fellows were walking downtown on Central Avenue, and out of the First National Bank building stepped an obviously wealthy gentleman. The first of our fellows said to the second, "See Banker Jones there? He cheated me out of more than $100,000."

"Good heavens! How did he do a thing like that?"

"He refused to let me marry his daughter."

+

"Is your good wife very economical?" Henry asked his pal.

"She certainly is, believe me. We have to do without everything I want."

+

One young wife went up to the window of bank teller Fred Rivers and said, "Please, I'd like to open a joint account with someone who has a lot of money."

If you're thinking of marriage, sir, you should make a little money first. Because after that, brother, you'll surely have to make a little money last!

+

The new bride was upset. "Henry, didn't you tell me that any bank would lend money on notes?"

"Well, yes, dear. That is, if you—"

"Well, the First National is a stinker. I showed the cashier all those sweet notes you wrote me before we left college, and he wouldn't lend me a penny on them."

+

After three hours of window shopping together, reading the many SAVE signs, husband turned to wifey and said: "Perhaps you have heard of another favorite way of saving also, dear. It's called putting money in the bank."

Fishing

"A husband," declared my sweet rib, right after I had returned from a long session of fishing without results, "is a jerk at one end of a pole waiting for a jerk at the other."

+

John had been nagged for days. Suddenly his inning came. "Why don't you still give me lovely presents," his Mrs. Demanded, "like you used to do before we were married?"

Said John, "Who ever heard of a fisherman feeding bait to a fish after he had caught it?"

They had fought hard with words. She thought to squelch him by saying, "Believe me, mister, there's better fish in the sea than the one I caught."

"There's better bait, too!" her man snapped back.

Friends

Mrs. Vaine was preening herself, and said to another woman at the party, "How do you like my new dress?"

"It's very sweet," the friend admitted.

"Henry gave it to me for my twenty-second birthday."

"Dear me, it surely has worn well."

+

"Run out to play with some of your little friends, dear," suggested mother.

"I can't," whined little dear. "I've only got one friend, and I *hate* him."

Girls

Mother found little Jewell crying. "What's the matter, dear?"

"My new shoes hurt me so."

Mother inspected them. "Oh. You have them on the wrong feet!"

"Wa-a-ah!" wailed Jewell even louder. "These are the only feet I have!"

Daddy's snoring sounded like the 5 p.m. trans-continental plane taking off. Presently he turned onto his side and abruptly the sound stopped. "Mother!" cried little Ellen, playing nearby. "Come quick! Daddy has killed his engine!"

+

Santa Claus had brought nine-year-old Madonna Marie a new wrist watch. An adult friend was admiring it: "How nice! And does it tell time, dear?"

"No," said Madonna. "You hafta look at it."

+

Daddy came home from work just before supper, and his beloved five-year-old daughter met him on the sidewalk. She was not smiling, so he asked why. "Is something wrong, sweetie?" said he.

"Yes," she declared. "All day long I've been having trouble with your wife."

+

Mother asked Susie: "Aren't you ashamed of being naughty? Do you know where bad little girls go?"
Said Susie: "Everywhere."

Graduation

The drugstore clerk was wrapping the gift. "Is this fountain pen to be a surprise graduation gift for your son, sir?" he asked.

"It certainly will be," papa nodded. "He's expecting a convertible."

Grandchildren

One elderly man wouldn't officially retire. He just went back to the office every morning anyway. But when he came home at night, little Walter, his grandson, would ply him with questions. After pumping the usual openers at him, Walter asked one day, "Grandfather, what do you do down at the office?"

"Nothing," said grandpa.

The lad considered that a moment, then asked, "Grandfather, how do you know when you are through?"

Grandparents

This was up north, and the winter was cold. This particular morning snow was on the ground, and at dawn a neighbor saw Grandpappy Doolittle out in his back yard in nothing but his nightgown, chopping wood.

"Hey, Grandpap," the neighbor yelled. "Are you crazy? Out here in your nightie in this zero weather?"

"Nope, I ain't," said grandpappy, without missing a swing of the axe. "For the past 76 years I have dressed by a warm fire every winter morning, and I'll be consarned if I'm gonna stop doin' it now!"

+

They say a fellow has reached old age when all he exercises is caution.

Cal Detwiler got news that his first-married child had a baby. Soon a friend asked, "Well, Cal, how does it feel to be a grandfather?"

"Don't mind it at all," confessed Cal. "In fact I rather like it. But I'm not sure I like the idea of being married to a grandmother."

+

Mr. Brown, aged 78, was very wealthy, very irascible, and very stingy. And he had an improvident nephew who lived in the hopes of inheriting his uncle's millions. But the years edged by and the old man wouldn't die. Then one day a friend met him on the street.

"Mr. Brown," said the friend, "I'm told your nephew is about to be married. Wouldn't it be nice if you did something to make the young fellow happy on that occasion?"

"You think it's my duty to do that?"

"Well, you know how it is. A wedding and all. And he's your only living kin."

"Very well," the old man agreed. "On the day of his wedding, I'll pretend to be dangerously ill."

+

"Do you have anything for gray hair?" a customer asked his druggist.

"Nothing," confessed the druggist, "but the highest respect, sir."

+

Middle age is that lamentable period when you must listen to advice from your children. And when the only clothes that fit are your newest.

Granddad came home from the movies in a mood. "How I do miss the good old days of silent pictures," he mused.

His wife was, as usual, in something of a mood too. "What was so grand about them?" she demanded.

"Well, in those days a man could watch a woman's mouth move for two hours without hearing a single word."

+

The married people's party drifted into talk about how couples first met. Some gave this version, some that. Finally the hostess asked Granddad Doakes how he first met Mrs. Doakes.

"I never met her at all," said he. "She overtook me."

+

"Shucks, I'm perfectly healthy," Granddad Hinks whined at the pool room meeting of his pals. "And the secret of my health is eating garlic three times a day."

Said one pal, "That's no secret."

Guests

Two kinds of neighbors come to your party — those who want to leave early, and those who don't. Unfortunately, they are usually married to each other.

+

Father, escorting guests to the door in the wee small hours: "It was certainly nice of you folks to drop in last night."

The Thanksgiving dinner was all set. Madam hostess and her several guests were at table. Susan the cook entered the dining room, bearing a huge roasted turkey on a silver platter. But suddenly — Susan tilted the platter a bit, and the turkey skittered across the floor.

The hostess, however, refused to be a victim of nerves. She had great poise and fine mental resources. She smiled at her guests reassuringly and said, "There, there, Susan, don't worry. Just take it back to the kitchen and bring in the other one."

+

Husbands can be stingy. This one ambled into the butcher shop and ordered ten cents' worth of T-bone steak. The butcher, a good family man, protested — "But look here, George, you got six children and a hungry wife. You can't feed them on the tiny scrap of meat I can sell you for a dime!"

Husband George stood his ground. "This here ain't for eatin'," said he. "We got company coming, after supper. This steak is just to put a good smell in the house."

+

Little Nancy was mother's helper. She helped set the table when company was due for dinner. Presently everything was on, the guests came in and everybody sat down. Then mother noticed something amiss. "Nancy dear," said she, "why didn't you put a knife and fork at Mr. Wilson's place?"

"I thought he wouldn't need them," explained Nancy. "Daddy said he always eats like a horse."

One night my neighbor had us all over to his house, and after dinner I got to talking about Texas. I felt that it was welcome talk, because it was cultural and inspiring. So I went on and on, happy thus to contribute to my neighbor's party. But after a while I paused to re-gather my thoughts for a moment, then I said, "Speaking about Texas makes me think of the time. . . ."

At which point my neighbor instantly butted in — "Heavens yes, you are so right! I had no idea it was getting so late. Good-night, all!"

+

The family had guests. When everybody had sat down for dinner, little Bolivar called from the bathroom, "Mother, there's only clean towels out. Shall I start one?"

Hair

Two kids were talking about a certain grown-up girl on the street, and one said: "Yeah, she's got long blonde hair with short black roots."

Hats

Ministers need never worry about women staying home on Sunday mornings to listen to radio or television preachers. Only in church can new hats be adequately displayed.

Mrs. Suddenrich went this morning to her milliner, one of the world's most famous. "I want," said she, "for you to create me an exclusive new model, right here and now."

"Instantly, madam? Right here?"

"Yes."

The milliner shrugged, but reached for a bolt of blue ribbon. With great dexterity he cut, twisted, turned and pinned, then placed the creation on her head and held up a mirror. It hadn't taken ten minutes. And the customer squealed with delight at the beauty of the new hat. "Fine!" she gushed. "How much is it, please?"

"Six hundred dollars."

"Six hundred? My, isn't that a mighty lot of money for three yards or so of plain, ordinary ribbon?"

"Madam," the milliner explained icily, "the *ribbon* is free!"

+

The missus: "Dovie Pie, I saw the sweetest little hat on display in the milliner's window today."

The mister (alias Dovie Pie): "Put it on, so I can see what it's like."

+

Doubtless you heard about the sweet and loving wife who went into a swanky men's shop to buy a hat for her husband. "I want a size 32," she burbled to Chet Goldberg, who was trying to wait on her.

"Uh — isn't that rather large for a hat, madam?" Chet suggested.

"No, I don't think so. You see, George wears a size 16 collar, and I estimate his head is about twice as big around as his neck."

Honesty

Mrs. Winslow came storming out the door, and glared at her husband. "Why do you always come out on the front porch when I'm singing?" she demanded. "Don't you like to hear me sing?"

"Tain't that, Thelma," explained her kind-hearted husband. "I just don't want the neighbors to think I'm beating you."

+

Any time you give your rib a blunt statement, mister, she's likely to make a point of it.

+

Sonny asked, "Daddy, how do they catch lunatics?" And Daddy let his feelings dominate enough to reply, "With fancy dresses, lipstick and pretty smiles, my son."

+

Romantic Mrs. Housewife, some years after her wedding: "Oh, William, when we were newlyweds you used to tickle my chin every night. Do it again, hmmm?"

The Mr.: "Sure. Which one?"

Housewives

They say it takes a brainy woman to earn her own living, but a smart one to let some man earn it for her.

The good housewife called up on the phone —
"Is this the Humane Society?" she asked.
"Yes, ma'am."
"Well, come at once. There's a vacuum cleaner
salesman sitting in a tree in our yard teasing our
dog."

+

Got up in the bright dawn yesterday, flexed my
muscles and told my beloved helpmeet, "I feel like
a two-year-old this morning."
Said she, "Horse or egg?"

+

We had to bury Horace Smith last
week. The poor reckless man agreed with
his wife when she looked at herself in
the mirror and said, "My hair is a mess."

+

The missus drove her family's car into the
repair shop. "Can you restore this fender quickly,
so my husband will never know?"
The mechanic nodded, but suggested, "I could,
yes, but why not let me just tinker it? Then you
can ask him in a day or two how he smashed it."

+

Mrs. Weevish had been called for jury duty. She
declined to serve because, said she, she did not
believe in capital punishment. The judge tried to
persuade her to stay. "Madam," said he, "this is
not a murder case. It is merely a case in which a
wife is suing her husband because she gave him
$2,000 to buy her a new fur coat and he lost it at
the race track instead."
"I'll serve," agreed Mrs. Weevish. "I could be
wrong about capital punishment."

Two neighborhood women were walking down the sidewalk one summer and came to the Henry Wood home. The yard grass was knee high. Milk bottles, papers, trash littered the porch. Through a front window, Henry's bare feet protruded slightly. He was sound asleep.

Said one of the ladies, "I see that Lottie Wood is still away."

+

Mrs. John Touchstone of Houston, Texas, had trouble with her laundry. It kept shrinking John's clothes — and nothing no nothing irritates a mate like a shrunken collar, sleeves or pajamas. In desperation his Jane tied a huge railroad spike to the next bundle of laundry with this note around it: "Shrink THIS, if you can!"

When the clean laundry was returned, an envelope had a note that read, "We could, and we did!" and glued to it was a small carpet tack.

+

"Wait, wait," the housewife yelled to the garbage truck. When it stopped, she ran to it and said, "Am I too late for the garbage?"

The driver replied, "No, ma'am. Climb right in."

+

The motorcycle officer stopped the speeding housewife and asked to see her driver's license. She dug into her purse. No results. She dug deeper. The officer waited solemnly. She rummaged some more. Finally she came up with a folder of cute little photos.

"Here, these are the pictures of my grandchildren," she said. "Look at those until I find my license. I know it's in here somewhere."

This was a rush hour in Chicago. The bus was crowded. It stopped, and three housewives, avidly talking to one another, squeezed down the front steps, blocking other passengers trying to get on. The tired driver (who should have known better) shouted, "Please use the rear door to leave the bus."

Instantly our three housewives stopped, chagrined, and got back on the bus, walked to the rear and left by that door!

They say the driver may regain his sanity in another six months.

+

You think a woman's voice doesn't change? Just listen when she's bawling out her husband, and the telephone rings.

Husbands

"Who's the boss in your home, Buck?" somebody asked T. J. "Buck" Arnold, a few years after he married pretty Georgia. Buck was an honest man. "Well, sir," he drawled, "Georgia naturally assumes control of the house and the children, the dog and the cat. But I'm allowed to say whatever I please to the goldfish."

+

A big, fat husband squeezing into his seat for morning coffee growled and said, "The same gent who invented the telephone booth also invented the breakfast nook."

"Any time you think life leaves *you* neglected, mister," said a friend to a householder, "just think of Whistler's father."

+

Another gentleman went into a bookstore and asked, "Have you any 'Do-It-Herself' books?"

+

"I see where Jasper finally married that lurid redhead," one neighbor reported to another.
"Boy! Whatever got into him?"
"Buckshot."

+

A friend met Jim Smith on the street. "Why is it you always look so seedy, but your wife is always elegantly dressed?" the friend asked.

"Because," explained Jim, who is a prototype of husbands everywhere, "Maggie dresses according to the figures in the fancy clothing shops, whereas I dress according to the figures in Smith & Company's ledgers."

+

Some husbands have become confirmed television addicts. The other night a man in my block turned on his radio by mistake, and thought he had gone blind.

"It wouldn't be so hard to save for a rainy day," growled the typical American husband, "if it didn't eternally keep on raining."

+

You are wrong if you think Benjamin Franklin was the first electrician. His work with lightning and the kite came long after Adam had furnished parts for the first loudspeaker.

+

One husband really wanted to drown his trouble. But she refused to go in swimming with him.

+

This husband was describing a girl he'd met. "She's not what you'd call unattractive," said he. "She's interesting, but it would be safe if you were talking to her when your wife walked in."

+

"Give a woman an inch," muttered this husband, "and she becomes a ruler."

Infatuation

Attack: "Ha! I was a fool when I married you!"
Counterattack: "Indeed yes. But I was so infatuated at the time that I couldn't notice it."

Jealousy

"I don't understand Jack Wilson," mused an acquaintance, reading the evening paper. *"He hasn't kissed his wife in ten years, but it says here he just shot another man who did."*

Jobs

The reporter came out to interview a typical wage earner. "I know from your boss," said the newspaper man, "that you have raised your family of nine children on only $50 a week. How did you do it?"

"Sh-h-h-h!" pleaded the man. "Don't let my wife hear you. I've told her I got only $45 a week."

+

Some families seem to have more money than brains. But not for long.

+

It's hard for any harassed wage earner to tell when his next break is coming. All he can do is hope that it won't be a fracture.

Kisses

Sophomore: "Would you call for help if I should try to kiss you?"

Freshman: "Why call anybody else? If you can't handle it by yourself, I'll help you."

The young people were needling grandfather. "They say girls were harder to kiss in your day, old timer?" one brash youth asked.

"Some," he admitted. "But it was much safer then."

"How so?"

"Well, no parlor sofa ever run over a cliff or smashed into a tree."

+

About 10:30 P.M. father came storming down into the living room and exclaimed, "I'll teach you to kiss my daughter, young sir!"

Said the boy, "Oh, thank you, sir, I wish you would. I'm not making much headway by myself."

+

"You never, never kiss me," whined the housewife's husband, "unless you want money."

"Isn't that often enough?" she demanded.

+

One teacher assigned a composition on "Things I'm Thankful For." Johnny's list included this: "My glasses. They keep the other boys from fighting me, and the girls from kissing me."

+

Neighbor: "I was sitting in my yard last night, and happened to see a boy trying to kiss your daughter."

Smith: "Did he succeed in kissing her?"

Neighbor: "No."

Smith: "Then it wasn't my daughter, for sure."

Mother, in one of those usual after-date sessions in her bedroom, said: "And so Wilbur finally kissed you unexpectedly."

"No," said daughter. *"Just sooner than I had expected."*

+

Some young men are insolent. This one was suddenly faced by an irate father who dashed into the living room after a moment of spying. Said pop, "I'll teach you to kiss my daughter!"

"Sorry," said the boy, "but you're too late. I've already learned how."

+

And then there's that classic about the right-eously indignant dad who dramatically exclaimed, "How is it I find you kissing my daughter, sir? How is it, I say?"

Replied the boy, "It's great, sir! Simply great!"

+

They say any boy is growing up when he'd rather steal a kiss than steal second base.

Love

Dimpled darling, married ten years: "Honey, will you still love me after I put on a few pounds?"

The mister: "Listen here, I promised for better or for worse, not through thick or thin."

"Darling," began the missus, cuddling up close to him in his easy chair, "do you love me still?"

Said the honest gent: "Yes, dear; better than any other way."

Maids

"Mabel," said Mrs. Jones to her maid one morning, in a moment of confession and worry, "I'm sure my husband is having an affair with his stenographer."

"I don't believe it," snapped Mabel, who was pretty herself. "You're just saying that to make me jealous, mum."

+

Mr. and Mrs. were having dinner, and the maid Fanny came in with soup and spilled it. Next she came in with coffee and spilled that. When she came in with beans and splashed them all over the husband, his wife spoke up: "Come to think of it, Henry, we forgot to give Fanny a present for her birthday yesterday."

+

The new maid was applying for a position and was asked to give references. "I couldn't list my last place," she confessed, "because the mistress and master were always quarreling."

"That must have been very unpleasant," said the prospective employer.

"Yes, mum. They was at it day and night, week in and week out. When it wasn't me and him quarrelin', it was me and her."

Mrs. Harris was reprimanding her maid. "Hilda, did you notice that I wrote your name in the dust on the piano?"

Said Hilda, "Yes, mum. And you misspelled it, too."

+

Statisticians report that one-third of all disastrous accidents of the household occur in the kitchen. This does not include those served at meals.

+

"The maid quit this morning," Mrs. Householder reported to her husband when he arrived from work. "She said you spoke in an insulting manner to her over the telephone."

"Good grief!" cried hubby. "Was that her? I thought it was you!"

+

The head of one household was a rather stern looking man. After a new maid had agreed to do the housework, she told a friend, "I doubt if I'm going to like working for him. He looks like the kind of boss who'll always be telling me what to do."

Manners

"Stop that reaching across the table, Junior!" snapped papa. *"Haven't you got a tongue?"*

"Yes, sir," this lad replied, meekly. *"But my arm is longer."*

"Stop that!" snapped father at dinner. "Son, you must learn table manners. You are nothing but a little pig at table. Do you know what a pig is?"

"Yes, sir. A hog's little boy."

Mistakes

Mama is working the crossword puzzle in the evening paper. Papa is smoking and reading the *Encyclopaedia Britannica*. Now how could such a harmless situation breed a family fight? Well, I'll tell you. Mama, poring over her puzzle, asks, "William, what is a female sheep?" Honest, earnest, loyal, loving William naturally replied, "Ewe."

+

Two women were at a party and, of course, were discussing a third woman. Lo! the third one herself entered the front door, and made quite an imposing production of her entry.

"Wasn't her husband a judge?" one of the gossips whispered.

"We all thought so," whispered back the other, "until he asked her to marry him."

+

A fellow named William Jones got a job as gardener for haughty Mrs. McBustle. She had one plot of especially choice flowers, and when she saw her new hired man at work she went up close, lifted her lorgnette and asked, "How is my sweet William doing?"

The man looked up from his knees, grinned, expectorated his tobacco and said, "If you're going to be like that, honey, just call me Bill."

My Adele and I had some folks in for dinner. One of them named Julian McCreary was an expert pianist. So while the roast cooked, Julian pounded our old parlor grand. He rolled out a whopping good nocturne. But the roast still wasn't done, so Julian turned to my farm-reared brother Buck Arnold, dozing in an armchair, and politely asked, "Would you like a sonata before dinner?"

Buck snapped awake and, always a gentleman, smiled and replied, "Yes, thank you, I would. I had a couple just before I left the house, but I could stand another."

Misunderstandings

It was past 3 a.m. and hubby was quietly sneaking in the front door. It didn't work. There she stood, waiting and glaring. He looked at her in resignation.

"So, home is the best place after all!" she began.

Sadly he shook his head and muttered, "No. But it's the only place open at this hour."

+

The minister was in good form. "Is there even one man in this audience," asked he, "that would just stand by and permit his wife to be slandered?"

In a back pew one meek little man finally stood up.

"What!" exclaimed the minister. "Do you really mean to stand there and admit that you would permit your own wife to be slandered?"

"Oh," said the meek husband. "I misunderstood you. I thought you said slaughtered."

McPherson was telling the boys about it. "While I was away from home last night, a burglar broke into my house."

"Imagine!" a friend exclaimed. "And did he get anything?"

"He did that. M'wife thought it was me coming in late."

+

He stumbled a little on the front porch. He found the door. He got the key in the lock. He got the door open. He got inside. There she stood. He beamed at her and said, "I bet you can't guess where I've been, sweetheart."

"I certainly can," snapped she. "But go on with your story."

+

"That lady got mad at me when I told her how well she looked in a bustle," lamented big Ben Dibble at the Kiwanis party.

"What's wrong with that?" asked Bill Boice.

"Plenty. She wasn't wearing a bustle!"

+

"Are you positive you'll love me after I get ugly and old?" whined the Mrs.

To which the Mr. bridled and asked, "Who says I don't?"

+

"They say you and your husband aren't getting along together very well," hinted Mrs. Snoop to a friend.

"That's a ridiculous rumor," the woman snapped. "Oh, Henry and I had a little argument, and I shot him. But that's as far as it ever got."

The scene here is the breakfast table. Mrs. Prototype Housewife is in her sleazy kimono. Her hair is in metal curlers. A mask of alleged "beauty" goo is on her face. Across the table is Mr. Typical Husband, dressed for the office, eating eggs. His newspaper is propped up between them so that the two can't possibly see one another.

"Why do you always read the paper like that at breakfast?" she asks.

"What gives you the idea that I *read* the paper?" he asks.

Money

Hubby was shooting back. "Ha! You accuse me of being a spendthrift, of extravagance. But I ask you, when have I ever bought one useless thing? Just name one!"

She did. "That fire extinguisher you bought two years ago. We haven't used it a single time."

+

The easterner was walking across the Texas ranch with the not-so-pretty but marriageable ranch girl. All around them were oil wells, flowing their wealth. "Darling," said the man, with remarkable honesty, "I worship the ground you walk on."

+

Esmeralda had been listening intently to her husband Bertram. He was pleased. "I'm happy to see you impressed by my lecture on economics and banking," said he.

"Yes," she nodded. "I'm enthralled at the fact that anybody can know so much about money without having any."

One particular night the boys were trying to amuse one another by talking money. The subject was "What I Would Do If I Had a Million Dollars."

Each man around the circle named his choices of spending. All but Tom. He hadn't spoken. Finally somebody asked, "How about you, Tom? Surely as a husband and father of nine youngsters, you'd know what to do with a million dollars."

He smiled wanly and said, "Yes. I believe I'd use it to pay my Christmas bills — at least as far as it would go."

Mother-in-Law

The good lady's son had married a while back and taken his bride clear across the nation to live in California. Somebody asked the lady if she had visited the young couple.

"No," said she. "I'm going to wait until they have their first baby."

"You mean you don't want to spend the money until then?"

"It isn't so much the money. But I have a feeling that a grandmother would be more welcome than a mother-in-law."

+

Young Dan Arnold was worrying out loud to some of his cronies. He had just been married, and he had a problem. "I can't decide what to call my mother-in-law," confessed Dan. "My own mother is still living, and so it wouldn't seem right to call my wife's mother 'Mother' too. I can't think what to call her."

"Just wait a little while," an older man counselled. "Pretty soon you can begin calling both of them 'Grandma.'"

Necking

"I caught my husband necking," one young matron said to another, close to tears. The second was no comfort. She replied, "Yes, I caught mine that way, too."

Neighbors

"I can say one thing for myself," declared Mrs. Snapp. "I have always tried to keep myself respectable."

"Speaking for *myself*," answered her neighbor, "I have never had to try."

+

One catty neighbor dropped in for a chat with one even cattier. Said the guest, "I feel low today. And whenever I'm in the dumps, I just get myself a new hat."

"That explains it," snapped her neighbor. "I've always wondered where you got them."

+

The neighborhood gossips had thoroughly studied the new neighbors. "He seems to be such a devoted husband," Mrs. Snooper reported to her own man. "He kisses her every time he leaves the house. He throws her kisses from the car, and waves good-bye. Why don't you do that, Henry?"

Henry: "Good grief, I haven't even met the woman yet!"

Next door neighbors were visiting over the back fence. Said one, "I thought I heard your wife quarreling with somebody last night, Hank."

"Naw," says Hank, "she was just scolding the dog."

"Oh, I see. Poor animal. I heard her say she was going to take the front door key away from him."

+

The family was bankrupt, and would be hauled into court the next day. The minister came to comfort the lady of the house. "It's all the neighbors' fault," said she.

"How is that?" the good man asked.

"Well, they were forever buying something or doing something we could not afford."

+

Love and brotherly affection can grow between neighbors. Thus: "I'm mighty sorry, pal," said one householder, "but my chickens got out and scratched up your new garden."

"Think nothing of it. My dog has since killed all your chickens."

Yes, I know. And I have since killed your dog."

+

Two neighbors were in the kitchen, looking at their two husbands out back together. Said one lady, "I wonder what in the world men talk about when they are together like that."

"Why, they talk about the same things we do," said her friend.

"Oh, aren't they horrible! They ought to be ashamed."

Mrs. McCatt met her neighbor downtown. "What a beautiful fur coat you have on this morning, dearie," she purred.

"Yes, my husband gave this to me for my 36th birthday."

"My, my, hasn't it worn well!"

+

Of course, there was the apartment dweller who turned off his radio one 11 p.m., only to discover that all the while he had been listening to his neighbors' quarrel.

+

Speaking of neighborly talk, Mrs. Watson and Mrs. Hale met one morning while sweeping their front walks. "You are looking mighty nice this fine morning," ventured Mrs. Watson.

Mrs. Hale sniffed and said, "I regret that I could not say as much about you."

Mrs. Watson shot right back, "If you were as big a liar as I am, you could."

+

Uncle Ben was out walking in the twilight, and the neighbors saw that he looked bad. They couldn't guess if he was sick or just returning from some sort of alcoholiday. So they asked him, "Why are you looking so thin and washed out, Uncle Ben?"

"Can't help it," said he. "My old wife's on a diet."

Little neighbors echo what they hear. Little Candace Collins on our street saw the furniture people move in some new items her mommy had bought. So she rushed across to invite us — "Come quick, and see our new drunken-fight chairs!"

+

"Is it true that your wife is a finished soprano?" somebody asked the long-suffering man.

"Not quite," said he. "But all the neighbors are working on it."

+

Says my neighbor-next-door: "That old gal was shy when you asked her age. Shy at least 15 years."

+

Most neighbor women seem to appreciate the simple things in life. Such as men.

+

The trouble with most neighbors, of course, is the fact that they have children. My neighbor next door is blessed — call it that — with four boys under nine years of age. Last week I dropped in for a moment. Four cowboys with guns were rushing around. One drew a lethal-looking cap pistol, shouted "Boom!", pulled the trigger, enjoyed the pop, and his mother dropped onto the couch. I waited. She lay there a long while, then winked at me and said, "Peace, it's wonderful. Playing dead is the only way I ever get any rest."

Snoopy Loopy came across the lawn to make inquiries of her neighbor. "Why are there so many chickens on your lawn this morning?" she asked.

"Uh, er," the neighbor thought fast. "They no doubt heard I was planning to lay a sidewalk today, and want to see how it's done."

Observations

Any husband needs tact. That's leaving unsaid the wrong things at the tempting moments.

+

Following an accident, a woman in our town was awarded $10,000 for the loss of a thumb. It was the one she had kept her husband under.

+

"It's strange," said Dick Smith, after supper one night, "how the biggest fools seem always to marry the prettiest women."

"Stop trying to flatter me," said Mrs. Smith.

+

"I hear tell that you and your Isabel had some words," Ray Petersen tactfully approached Bill Norris, on the golf course.

"Yeah, I had some," Bill agreed, "but I've still got them. I didn't get a chance to use them."

Ray smiled in sympathy, then asked, "Now come on, tell the truth. Don't you really like talkative women as well as the other kind?"

Said Bill, "What other kind?"

Do you dear hearts and gentle people know why a rooster crows so early in the morning? It's because he's afraid to open his mouth after the old hen wakes up.

Old Age

Old age needs very little. But it needs that little very much.

+

Grandfather Dewey Swihart, a benign gentleman getting no younger every day, went to his doctor. "I've got a pain in my left arm," he complained.

The doctor took out his stethoscope, his microscope, his stereoscope, and his Cinemascope. He examined Uncle Dewey thoroughly. Then he snapped his instruments back into his bag and gave his diagnosis. "Sorry, Mr. Swihart, there's nothing medical science can do for you. Truth is, your arm pains you simply because of old age."

"That doesn't make sense," Grandpap Swihart exclaimed. "My right arm is just as old as my left one, and it doesn't hurt at all!"

+

The funeral was over, but the eager-beaver mortician always had an eye out for business, so he waited near the front door. A very old looking man filed out, and the mortician asked, "How old are you, sir?"

"I'm 98 years old," said the old man.

"Hmmmm," purred the business man. "Hardly worth going home, is it?"

One day a hearing aid salesman called on elderly Mr. Wilson, keeper of a country store.

"Don't need one," Mr. Wilson replied. "I got a cheaper gimmick." He reached under his counter, got a little short piece of wire and wound it from his coat pocket to one ear.

"But that has no connections of any sort," the salesman protested. "No microphone or battery or anything."

"Don't need anything else," Mr. Wilson explained. "Whenever people see this wire on me, they all talk louder."

+

Three fine old boys were taking their ease in the nursing home, rocking and resting and waiting.

"If my time came to die today," one ventured, "I think I'd choose to jump off a high cliff."

Nobody else spoke for 15 minutes or so. Then the second old timer, aged about 87, said, "If it was my time to go, I'd choose to fly up 50,000 feet in a jet plane then jump out."

After nearly half an hour of silence, the third one, aged 92, spoke up. "If it was my time to die, I'd choose to be shot by a jealous husband."

+

We do not count a man's years until he has nothing else to count.

—Emerson.

+

An old timer? He's a man who can remember back when a naughty child was taken to the woodshed instead of to the psychiatrist.

The newspaper reporter had been sent out to interview Old Man Hornswaggle on his 90th birthday, and things went along smoothly enough. "Yes, sir," the old man said, "I'm mighty proud to say I ain't got an enemy on earth."

"Congratulations, sir," nodded the reporter. "That's a beautiful feeling to have."

"Yep. The last enemy I had petered out about two years ago."

Politicians

Two men met on the train, and discovered that they were old neighbors who hadn't seen one another for quite a while. "To tell you the truth, Sam," said one, "I haven't been around. I been in prison, and it's sure going to be hard to face old friends back home."

"I know just how you feel," his friend said, sympathetically. "I face the same thing. I'm just returning home from Congress."

+

The time came when Charles Evans Hughes was elected governor of New York for the second time, but it had been a hard campaign. Afterward, a neighbor came to visit him in the executive mansion, and was highly impressed with it.

"Mighty fine place you have to live in here, Mr. Governor," the friendly neighbor said.

"Thank you," said Mr. Hughes. "But I had a hard time getting the landlord to renew my lease this year."

"Politics makes strange bedfellows," said neighbor Bayless in my yard last night. "And yet, they soon become accustomed to the same old bunk."

+

One of my good neighbors entered politics. One night he went down into the industrial district to make himself a campaign speech, and about 11 p.m. came to relax in my yard. I asked him: "How did your audience react, Sam? Did they applaud that part where you said you never had bought a single vote for office?"

Sam shook his head. "No. A few old ladies applauded, but most of the men appeared to lose interest right there. Several of them even walked out on me."

Preachers

Aaron Powers, a preacher with several children, took them all on vacation in a huge trailer house. After ten days their next door neighbor allegedly telegraphed the family: HAVING A WONDERFUL TIME. PLEASE STAY AS LONG AS YOU CAN.

+

In Laguna Beach, California, a Christian Science member attended the Presbyterian church where Dr. Dallas Turner preached. After a few weeks some good member asked the woman if she wouldn't like Dr. Turner to call.

"I should say not" the woman exclaimed. "I don't want him hounding me about joining his church. Furthermore, I would like you to know I don't believe a thing he says. But I just love the way he says it!"

The big First Presbyterian Church of Phoenix, Arizona, has a continuing art exhibit in its beautiful parlor, serving local artists without charge. One Sunday just after worship service, the pastor overheard a group of older artists sneering at the works of a young painter which had been hung that month. "But I like him very much," the pastor put in, gently.

"Hah!" one of the older painters snorted. "What is it you like about him?"

"For one thing, he doesn't show off," said the pastor. "I find that to be very unusual in a man without talent."

+

The prominent pastor and the prominent obstetrician, friends in private but enemies in public, happened to meet when visiting a Rotary Club.

"Well, well, preacher!" the obstetrician boomed, grinning. "Haven't seen you in months. And are you still delivering those little bits of wisdom in your pulpit?"

"Yes," the preacher replied affecting humility. "And yourself now — are you still delivering those little bits of people in your hospital?"

+

The Arkansas mountain minister told his people that he had a "call" to go to another church. A church officer asked how much more pay he had been offered.

"Four hundred dollars," said the parson.

"Can't blame you for going, pastor," said the officer, an expert on Saturday night poker. "But four hundred bucks ain't a *call*, that's a raise."

One day a pastor happened to take a short cut behind a warehouse, and came onto four of his male parishioners sitting on the ground apparently playing poker.

"Mike," he chided one, "you are playing poker against the law!"

"Not *me*, your riv-rence," Mike protested. "I was just sitting here with my friends."

"Then *you* are gambling, Terence," the minister pointed to the next man.

"Never a bit, sir. I was discussing politics."

"Then you, Aloysius!"

"Not at all, sir. I'm just resting here, waiting for a friend."

Exasperated, angry, the preacher turned to the fourth man. "Well then, Patrick, you are bound to be playing poker!"

Pat's innocence was a thing to behold. He spread his hands, shrugged and asked, "With who, your riv-rence?"

+

One good pastor addressing the Rotary Club in our town, lapsed momentarily from his usual calm dignity and blew his top:

"How ridiculous can you fathers get? You buy your son, a Jaguar, add Sidewinder tires, put a tiger in his tank, then insist that he drive defensively!"

+

Pastor Vogel took his watch in to Deacon Otto Schmieder, the distinguished jeweler, and said, "Repair it, please. I have all the faith in the world in this watch, but faith without good works is dead."

The Kiwanis Club was celebrating the eightieth anniversary of one of its member's businesses, and the speaker made quite a thing of it. "Is there anyone else here who represents a firm that has been in business as long as eighty years?" he orated.

A preacher arose and said, "I have that honor, sir."

+

After a hard day of counseling the high school members of his congregation, the Rev. Bill Vogel came home tired and said grimly to his wife, "You know something? The best substitute for experience is being sixteen."

After the church session had discussed financial problems at length, the Rev. Aaron Powers stood up and summarized it for them:

"As I understand it, gentlemen, if our outgo exceeds our income, the upkeep will be our downfall."

+

The Methodist bishop was walking beside the lake with his two beautiful daughters, and came onto an angler. He asked, "Is the fishing good, sir?"

"Fair. Are you a fisherman too?"

Said the bishop, "I am a fisher of men."

The angler looked appreciatively at the girls and said, "Well, you have mighty fine bait there!"

+

"We lost four of our college-age girls to the Methodists recently," lamented Presbyterian pastor Aaron Powers. "Everybody on our own church staff is married, but the Methodists recently hired a new single and handsome young assistant minister who played halfback for the University of Southern California."

Dr. Bill McCorkle, former minister in St. Louis, originated an idea for helping church ushers. In the sanctuary he was going to install a mechanical contrivance whereby he could press a button and have the back pews move quietly around to the front without disturbing the worshipers in them.

+

Preachers are poorly paid. One of them went to a carnival. There he saw a strong man stand on a platform, squeeze a lemon with one hand until it was dry, then challenge all comers. "If you can get one more drop of juice out of this lemon," said the performer to the public, "I will pay you $10."

Four big muscular fellows came up and tried it. All failed. Then our preacher came up, took that lemon and squeezed six drops out. "Who are you?" demanded the strong man.

Said he, "I'm the Scotch Presbyterian minister."

Proposals

"Please, Jane, will you marry me?" Bob pleaded.
"No. But I will always admire your good taste."

Punishment

"You needn't cry, little fellow," the kindly stranger comforted. "You'll get your reward in the end."

"T-that's what I'm w-worried about," sniffed the lad. "I always do."

Mother had been punishing Junior, and now was explaining to father: "He said some naughty words. I washed his mouth out with soap and he said them again, but I couldn't blame him this time."

+

The main trouble with many of our modern smart kids is that they aren't permitted to smart in the right place.

+

Mama bear was holding baby bear across her knees and walloping him for carelessness. "I don't like to punish you, son," said she, "but it's better for me to do it than to have a hunter tan your hide."

Questions

Butch Smith was pounding out his piano practice. It sounded like murder, but it was loud and zestful. The door bell rang, and Butch answered. "Is your mother home, sonny?" a salesman asked.

Butch gave him a sardonic glance and said, "What do *you* think?"

+

Susie: "Mother, who is my nearest relative?"
Mother: "Why, I am, dear."
Susie: "Are you my closest relative, too?"
Mother: "No, dear. Your father is."

Pop was tired. He had been through a hard day at the office. Now he was lying on the couch at home trying to relax and rest, but his little son peppered him with questions. Next to last question was, "Daddy, what do you do down at the office all day?"

"Nothing!" *yelled fed-up daddy.* "Nothing at all!"

The lad considered that seriously, then asked the last: "Daddy, how do you know when you have finished?"

+

The phone rang and little Patsy answered. No, daddy wasn't home, in fact nobody was home but Patsy herself. "Please tell daddy that Mr. Jones called," said the man.

"Wait till I get me a pencil," asked Patsy. Then she came back on and asked, "How do you spell Jones?"

"J-o-n-e-s."

Silence held for awhile. Then Patsy meekly asked, "How do you make a J?"

+

Devastating commentary on landlords came from little Vicki and Mildred, playing in the yard. One pretended she was a lady who had come to rent the other's playhouse.

"Do you have any parents?" asked the owner.

"Yes, I do, madam. Two of them."

"Well, then I'm sorry, but I can't rent to you. We never rent to children with parents. They are much too destructive and noisy."

"Boy oh boy, don't you ever stop asking questions?" one father raved. *"I just wonder what would have happened if I had dared ask as many questions when I was your age."*

"If you had," his son replied, *"maybe you'd now be able to answer some of mine."*

+

Sweet little Miss Sue Zane Bell and family were taken from the farm to New York City for the first time. They were enjoying all the sights. Finally they came to the Empire State Building and got on the elevator. As the indicator — and Sue Zane's tummy — indicated floor after floor zooming by and they passed the 55th, the child murmured, *"Daddy, does God know we are coming?"*

Reason

"The one thing that women dread most about their past," suggests George Hall, "is its length."

+

This missus was fed up. "Just suppose we housewives should go on strike," she suggested to her man.

"Go ahead," said hubby, beaming. "I know a cute blonde strike breaker."

+

"Dry up, woman!" strong-willed Mr. Jones yelled at his wife. *"If you don't stop this nagging, I'll let my insurance lapse!"*

Said the harried husband, greatly depressed: "Everything has gone wrong. I see no hope. My house just burned down, my daughter eloped with a scoundrel, my wife has left me, the bank is foreclosing on my mortgage, and the Tigers lost two to three in the ninth. Imagine that — two to three in the ninth!"

+

"Probably the only female on earth who can tell you what's in her bag," says Arthur Lee, "is a lady kangaroo."

Recreation

Tom had bowled every Tuesday night for years, but one Tuesday night he never returned home. Just disappeared. Seven years passed. Then one Tuesday morning Tom returned home.

His Martha was overjoyed, so she began at once calling friends to come over. "Why are you doing that?" Tom demanded.

"Why, I'm having a home-coming dinner for you," she explained, "and a big party afterward."

"Good grief, woman!" he shouted. "Not on my bowling night!"

+

"My sweet wife says if I don't give up playing poker she's going to leave me," reported Joe Smith.

"That's tough," his old friend sympathized.

"Sure is," agreed Joe. "I'll miss her a lot."

Religion

*An eastern tourist was visiting the arid desert world
of southern Arizona. "Do you never get any rain
here?" he asked.*

*The native Arizonan looked thoughtful for a long
moment, then said, "Well, sir, do you recollect that
story in the Bible, where it says Noah built an ark
when it rained forty days and forty nights?"*

"Well, yes, of course," nodded the tourist.

"We got half an inch that time."

+

A lady once asked Sir Winston Churchill
if he were a pillar of the church.

"Not exactly, madam," said he. "I am
more like a flying buttress — I support it
from the outside."

+

In the summer of 1968, when politics scorched
America, a very pretty young Baptist was roaring
down the highway in her car, doing 90 miles per
hour. A handsome young cop took out after her. Both
were from the same church.

Walking toward the speeding cars were two men,
known to be Methodists. In her excitement, the girl
hit them. One tore right through her windshield
into the car. The other was knocked far out of sight.

"Oh dear me," the poor girl cried. "I am so sorry.
Whatever can we do now?"

"Well, Pansy," the young Baptist cop drawled, admiring her beauty as well as her religion, "I will give
this man a ticket for forcible entry, and the other one
a ticket for leaving the scene of an accident."

One of those tramp steamers that have villainous crews was in trouble. It had struck a mine and was about to sink. The crew, including the captain, was made up of thugs and outlaws in general, but they now faced doom.

The captain spoke up. "Can anybody here sing a hymn?"

Nobody could. So he asked, "Well, then, who can say a prayer?"

Nobody could do that, either. The captain looked at his men with obvious disgust and growled, "Well, hang it, we got to do *something* religious. So I will pass among you and take up a collection."

+

Old Man Conway came to the church social with vile likker on his breath. Miss Lucretia Weems, a fussy old maid, sniffed audibly and said, "Whiskey nauseates me."

"Too bad, ma'am," he said sympathetically. "You may have to do what a friend of mine did — quit the stuff."

+

At Quincy, Ohio, one old favorite hymn got overworked at a prayer meeting, reports Miss Edna Jones. Aunt Emma, always present in spite of her twelve children, always led the singing. She opened with "Sweet Hour of Prayer." Well and good.

But her brother happened to come five minutes later and asked for it, so the folks sang it again.

Then a faithful old elder came in ten minutes late, and you just can't offend an old saint like that. *He* wanted to sing "Sweet Hour Of Prayer!" Happily, a hymn so beloved never wears thin.

Resignation

"Do you permit your wife to have her own way?" I asked Loren Pedrick.

"No," he admitted. "She has it without my permission."

+

A married couple had stopped at one of those drugstore scales, where you drop in a penny. Hubby got on, put in the coin, and the works moved. Out dropped a little fortune card. Wifey picked it up and read, "You are a charming personality, a leader of men, a citizen of high character and intellect, attractive to members of the opposite sex." Then she glanced at the big dial and added, "Goodness, it has your weight wrong too."

+

Joe Doakes has insomnia so bad he can't even fall asleep when Mrs. Doakes is talking to him.

+

"Do you ever quarrel with your missus?" a friend asked poor Mr. Weemish.

"Used to," he admitted, "until we both discovered I was wrong."

Romance

"I'm sure you and he will have a lot in common," said co-ed Rosie to her roommate concerning a blind date. "He is single, too."

Two girls were walking across the campus rather late at night. Mary whispered to Helen, "Say, I'm sure there's a man following us. Whatever shall we do?"

Said Helen rationally, "Let's match for him."

+

Brash young Boliver had at last come to Judy's father to ask about marrying her. "Of course," he began, "I know it's only a formality, but we thought it would please you."

Father swelled. "And who, may I demand young sir, told you that asking for my consent to Judy's marriage was a mere formality?"

"Judy's mother, sir."

+

Young Wilbur's parents were none too happy about his choice of a girl friend while attending college, and they tried tactfully to say so. "But shucks," Wilbur explained, "Gloria's the best girl I can get with the kind of car we have."

+

"I caught my fiancé flirting," announced Ruth, home from a date.

"I understand," Mom nodded. "That's the way I caught your father, too."

+

A handsome young Eskimo drove his dog team all the way down to San Diego College just to tell his girl he loved her. That's a lot of mush.

Perhaps the most popular elderly man of his time was William Jennings Bryan. One day a photographer — or maybe it was an artist — was doing his portrait, and asked, "Mr. Bryan, why do you always wear your hair hanging over your ears?"

The great statesman smiled benignly and explained, "When I was courting Mrs. Bryan, she didn't like the way my ears stuck out. So to please her, I tried to cover them with my hair."

"But that was many years ago, sir."

"Oh, yes," Mr. Bryan smiled again. "But you see, the romance is still going strong."

+

One tactless young man wrote to her thus: "Dear Sue: You'll have to excuse me, I'm getting horribly forgetful. I'm sure I proposed to you last night after the dance, but I forget whether you said yes or no."

Sue was not offended, however. She wrote back her courteous reply: "Dear Herkimer: It was sweet of you to write. I understand, too, because I'm also forgetful. I *knew* I had said 'no' to somebody last night, but I had completely forgotten who."

+

The young lady felt sure that if she got married the old folks would mope about it for years. So when her boyfriend went in to ask father, she worried. Finally the young fellow came out. "What did father say when you told him you would take me out of his home?" the girl demanded.

"He was upset at first," her lover admitted. "But I squared things with a good cigar."

Savings

The biggest obstacle our family has to saving money is the neighbors. They're always buying things we can't afford.

+

Two little kids were giving serious discussion to the important subject of piggy banks. "I believe it is childish to save money this way," one spoke up. "It would seem to encourage children to become misers."

"Yes, but that's not all," agreed his five-year-old friend. "It also causes parents to stoop to bank robbery."

+

Any family man is willing to agree that a fool and his money are soon parted. What really puzzles him, though, is how the fool got the money in the first place.

+

This was in arithmetic, and the teacher asked, "William, assume that your mother could save twenty dollars a week for twenty weeks. What would she then have?"

Willie knew. "A new set of living room furniture."

+

Joe's thrifty friend saw fit to ask Joe, "Have you something put aside for a rainy day?"

"Yes," said good old Joe. "An umbrella."

"You can save enough on your food bill to pay for this new refrigerator," the salesman assured Mrs. Housewife.

"We are already paying for a washing machine by the laundry bills we save," said she. "And a car with the bus fare we save. I just don't see how we can afford to save any more money right now."

School

The man on the corner told his cronies his little boy had trouble with eczema. "Boy, how'd he get it?" a friend asked.

"He hasn't got it," explained papa. "He couldn't spell it in school."

+

It was homework time, and mother was helping Bobby with his arithmetic. "Now how much is seven and five?" she asked.

Bobby's brain labored, and he replied, "Eleven."

"Not bad, not bad at all," commended father sitting nearby. "He only missed it by two."

Shopping

This was in Goldwater's swanky department store. The pretty saleslady was admiring the dress she had put on the customer. "My, my, dear lady, that's the most perfect fit I have ever seen!"

"Drop by my house on the first of next month," the customer suggested, "and see the one my husband throws when he gets the bill."

Hubby was reading the morning paper at break-fast. Unlike most such men, he also was aware of his wife's existence. Said she, "If the weather's decent today, dear, I want to go shopping. What does the paper say about it?"

And he pretended to read: "Heavy rain, sleet, snow, hail, coupled with a tornado that'll turn into a long, freezing blizzard."

+

The lady of the house spoke: "Henry, on your way home from work tonight, please stop in the department store and bring me two yards of material matching this sample of silk."

Her man asked, "You mean there at that front counter, where that red-haired cutie with the big blue eyes waits on us?"

The lady said, "Oh, on second thought, just let it go. It's unfair of me to expect you to do my shopping after you've had a hard day at the office."

+

Said Joe to his neighbor Bill: "My wife got to dreaming last night. Dreamed she was a million-aire's wife."

Bill: "Hah! Mine gets the same notion when she goes shopping."

+

The office clerk entered the boss' office and said, "Sir, may I have the rest of the day off to go shopping with my wife?"

"Certainly not," snapped the boss.

The man beamed and said, "Thank you very much, sir."

Silence

Little Susan came in and reported, "They are going to teach us domestic silence at school."

Said mother, "Don't you mean domestic science?"

Said father, "Let the child alone. There's an off chance she means what she's saying."

+

Father came home beat from a hard day at the office. When he had settled in the living room with his shoes off, mother said, "Our daughter has arranged a little piece for the piano."

"Fine!" said father. "It's high time we had a little peace around here."

+

The time is 2 a.m. Pop the apartment dweller has been trying without success to sleep, so he gets up, climbs the stairs to the apartment above his, and knocks on the door where the party is in full swing. His upstairs neighbor opens, smiling happily and somewhat blearily.

"Say, didn't you hear me pounding on the ceiling?" Pop demands.

" 'S'all right, neighbor. Keep pounding," Mr. Upstairs replies. "We been making a lot of noise up here, too."

Sisters

The same 15-year-old sister one day in a moment of romantic ecstasy said, "The man I marry must be a hero."

"Oh," big brother put in, generously, "you're not as bad as all that."

Big brother Robert knew everything. Big brothers often do. Anyhow, on this occasion Sister got an invitation to a party, and at the bottom of it were the mysterious letters R.S.V.P.

"I wonder what they mean?" said Sister.

So Robert loftily explained, "They mean — 'Rush in, Shake hands, Vanish Pleasantly.' "

Sons

Dad was trying to raise his son properly. "My boy," said he, "I never kissed a girl until I met the one who was to become your mother. Will you be able to say as much to *your* son?"

"Sure, Dad," sonny replied. "But probably not with such a straight face."

+

"How much will it cost me to get married, Dad?" Sonny asked.

"Depends on two factors," Dad replied. "How much you have, and how long you will live."

+

One particular son had managed to get his degree, but that was in June and this was now December. Meanwhile he hadn't turned a lick of work, just loafed around the house. Papa decided to lay it on the line for him. "My boy," he began, expansively, "I am proud of what I achieved. Why, when I was your age, I was assistant hod carrier for a gang of masons building a brick wall. I worked hard and diligently."

Sonny nodded. "Mighty proud of you, Pater. Proud of your pluck. Why, if it hadn't been for you, I might have to start doing something of the sort myself!"

Sonny was learning about life. "Why can't men have more than one wife, Dad?" he asked.

"Son, as you grow older you will learn that each state has laws to protect men unable to protect themselves."

+

Said Dad to his son entering business, "Too many of these prominent family trees you hear about were started by grafting."

+

Six-year-old Billy Preston was gazing at the goldfish in its bowl, and presently turned to his daddy and asked, "How can you tell a boy fish from a girl fish?"

"You tell by the worms used to catch them with," Daddy explained. "If you bait your hook with a male worm, you catch a female fish. If you bait with a female worm, naturally you catch a male fish."

Billy considered that, then asked, "But how do you tell the difference between a male and a female worm, Daddy?"

That's where Daddy revealed his inner self. "Don't ask me that," he growled. "I only know about *fish.*"

+

No matter how big a fall guy father is, he's no fool; often he can even outsmart his own kids. One day a dad's son came home after his freshman year at college, and was boasting of his mathematical knowledge. "Math is infallible," said the boy. "It is an absolutely exact science."

Pop thought a moment, then said, "Consider this — if I have one object, and you have one

object, and we exchange, we will each have one
object still. Is that right?"

"Sure," sonny agreed. "If you exchange equally,
you'll always have the same number. Can't beat
that kind of arithmetic."

"But," said father, "if I have one idea and you
have one idea, and we exchange, we each have two
ideas. Don't we, son?.... I say, don't we, son?....
Son, wake up; do you still think mathematics is
all-important?"

Teachers

Did you hear about the cross-eyed teacher? She
had no control over her pupils.

+

Some years ago Mr. John Owens, a man of
honor, was riding the bus one Saturday morning
when a pretty young woman across the aisle smiled
at him and said, loud enough for all the bus to
hear, "Aren't you the father of one of my
children?"

John blushed then sputtered, "M-Me? Madam, I
— how would I — I mean, I couldn't say. That is,
I—"

The other passengers were listening, but the
young lady didn't notice. She just went on: "I'm
sure you are. I teach fourth grade at Madison
School, and I met you and Mrs. Owens at a P.T.A.
meeting."

Traveling

One family, a man and his wife, had been rolling along normally on their vacation trip. After a sharp curve, a motorcycle cop flagged the man down. "Hey, your wife fell out of your car back yonder around the bend," said he.

The tourist looked relieved. "Oh, so that's what it was. I was afraid I had suddenly lost my hearing."

+

Not all picturesque mountain villages court the good will and good dollars of tourists; some have pride. One fast-driving papa pulled up to a store as he approached a village in the Ozarks and asked, "Do you have a speed law through here?"

"Nawp," said the merchant, from his front porch chair. "People like you can't git through here any too fast for us."

Question asked by every proud householder about to drive down to see the folks on his vacation: How do the birds know I have just had my car polished?

+

"Don't stop here," ordered the back seat wife as Henry slowed down in front of a motel with a vacancy sign showing. "If it has a vacancy it can't be much of a place to stay."

+

Sign at the entrance to a western village:
Our speed limit is 30 miles an hour. For faster driving the fine is $5 per extra mile. Select a speed you can afford.

One traffic cop was firm. "Pull over to the side of the road," he ordered from his motorcycle. The harassed papa at the wheel obeyed, and the cop went on: "It's midnight, and you don't have any tail lights."

Papa got out, walked to the rear of his car, and began to make queer noises. They sounded like racking sobs mixed with cries of astonishment, and were so impressive that the cop felt a twinge of pity. "Oh, maybe it's not all that bad," said he. "The fine shouldn't be very high."

"It's not the tail lights I miss," explained papa. "I'm just wondering where I lost my house trailer!"

+

Another family vacation driver was in trouble. "Just how did you happen to lose control of your car, sir?" the investigating officer asked.

Said the man, "My wife was asleep on the back seat."

+

Officer Hannigan flagged down another tourist family. "May I see your license," he ordered.

The harassed father nodded wanly and said, "Okay, officer. Campfire, hunting, fishing, or marriage?"

+

They had driven and driven and driven, with nothing to break the nighttime monotony except "No Vacancy" signs on motels. And they were very sleepy people. Finally, mother thought she would encourage papa, who was driving. So she said, "I know we'll find a place with a vacancy soon, honey. People are starting to get up."

Truth

One old timer was sounding off in typical fashion — remembering, way back when. Some younger men were politely listening. "Yep," said the old man, "I was always a good boy when I was young. I only got one whipping in my life, and strange to say, that was for telling the truth."

"Well," murmured one listener, "it cured you."

+

"Daddy," began a little eight-year-old girl, "does m-i-r-a-g-e spell marriage?"

"Yes, darling."

+

Art Wyss the druggist happened to meet one of his customer friends on the street. "Say, Fred," Art asked, "that mud pack I sold you for your wife to put on her face — did it improve her appearance?"

"Yes, it did for all of that night," Fred nodded. "Then she washed it off."

+

The doctor's phone rang and he answered. "Come to my house, Doc," a man pleaded. "My son has swallowed a fountain pen."

"Good heavens!" exclaimed the sympathetic doctor. "I'll be right there. What are you doing about it in the meantime?"

"Why, in the meantime I'm using a pencil," said the father.

Vacations

Back to normalcy now — let us consider the sweet young bride who hadn't been around much, and who was starting on her first vacation. Her husband warned her to be very careful of strangers and not let some strange man mislead her in any manner. She was duly cautious. Sure enough, at the big railroad station a strange man — actually the porter — asked her where she was going.

"To San Francisco," she replied.

So he escorted her to the train about to depart for California. She peered at him out the window, and when the train was safely rolling, she called back to him — "I fooled you, you old masher! I'm really going to see my mother up in Maine!"

+

"I truly wish we had brought the television set along, dear," said hubby, helping the porter load their luggage onto the train.

Replied his wife, "Don't be silly, Henry. Why ever would we want to take the television set?"

"Because," said he, humbly, "I left the tickets on it."

+

The vacationing man had just whammed his car into one driven by a woman. The investigating officer was very sympathetic. "If I were you, sir, I'd settle," he suggested. "Because when you get to court, it will be just your word against thousands of hers."

The zoo keeper went with his family on vacation, and was having a marvelous time until a telegram arrived from his assistant back on the job: EVERYTHING OKAY HERE EXCEPT THE BIG MONKEY SEEMS TO BE PINING FOR A COMPANION. PLEASE ADVISE WHAT TO DO UNTIL YOU RETURN.

+

Bob Creamer learned two things while his wife Jane was on a visit back East at her mother's: batching gets lonely, and a month is a mighty long time.

+

"Do you remember where you met your wife?" a friend asked Joe Smith.

"Yes, in a travel agency. I was trying to decide where to spend my vacation, and she was a last resort."

+

A young husband sent his beautiful young wife to Laguna Beach, California, for a vacation. Two weeks later she sent him a photo of herself resting languidly under her umbrella in front of the breakers. A note with it said that she was very lonely for him but he was not to worry, inasmuch as she didn't want to distract his mind from his work. Hubby was mighty proud of that letter and photo. He showed it downtown to all the boys. He drooled over it when he went to bed about 11 p.m. that night.

Then he got to thinking, and about midnight he suddenly left his bed, telephoned her at Laguna and demanded, "Honey, who took that picture of you?"

A fine family from Edinburgh, Scotland, was on vacation in the Canadian north woods. Sandy had hired a competent outdoorsman guide. After a little walk, Sandy suddenly stopped, pointed across a stream and said to the guide, "Look yon! What can that enor-r-rmous creature be?"

"That's a moose, sir," said the guide.

"A moose indeed!" Sandy was astonished. "And now I am wondering what your Canadian r-r-rats must look like!"

+

A Yankee was on vacation in East Texas, where he had some family roots. But he got confused, and pulled up at a little store. Elmer Barefield was sitting on the front porch of the store, enjoying life in the shade. The stranger addressed him — "Sir, I am trying to find the town of Minden, Texas. Could you tell me how to get there?"

"Mister," said Elmer, smiling, "don't move an inch!"

+

"Can't afford for both of us to go to Arizona this winter," growled busy Bill Doakes to his wife. "But you go, dear, and it will be vacation enough for me."

Vanity

Flies had swarmed into the house. Pat and his wife Judy were swatting them. "How many have you killed?" Judy asked presently.

"Nine males and seven females," replied Pat.

"Gollee, how can you tell the males from the females?"

"Easy," ribbed Pat. "The seven were on the mirror."

Youth

Vivacious Jeannie Pipsaire gave a demonstration of double baton twirling after Youth Meeting in her church one Sunday night. A few adults protested because it had happened in a church.

"That's just fine!" ruled the pastor emphatically. "Jeannie also lead the devotionals tonight, in case you didn't know. She's cheering for the right team. What cheering have you done lately?"

+

"I'm two-thirds married to Jerry," said Rosie to her friend.

"Really? How is that?"

"I'm willing, and the preacher is willing."

+

"Our growing daughters never did get by with much mischief in our home," my wife told our pastor. "I understood them too well; once I myself was a teen-aged teen-ager."

"Many a young woman who has stayed out playing with fire," warned the Rev. Albert Hjerpe, "has ended up cooking over one."

+

The Rev. Charles R. Ehrhardt, traveling around the world on a mission study, was cornered in India by a locally famous radio announcer who also was a nature-lover.

"Dr. Ehrhardt," the interviewer asked, "what do you consider to be America's most valuable wild life?"

In complete accuracy the good minister replied, "Our teen-agers."

+

"Daddy," began the ever-questioning small son, "what do you call a man who brings you in touch with the spirit world?"

"A bartender, son."

Wives

My own wife is a very capable woman. She can get home 10 minutes before I do and look as if she had been waiting there for me all evening.

+

"Why on earth did you tip that check room girl a whole dollar?" hissed the wife as they left the night club.

"Did you see her smile?" papa asked. "And just look at the fine hat she gave me."

They say any man's life is divided into two main parts — when she hangs on his neck, and when she jumps on it.

+

Helpful Home Hint for Householders: To prevent injury to thumb or other fingers when using a hammer, get your wife to hold the nail.

+

"Say, Bill," a neighbor said over the hedge one evening, *"your wife has changed. She used to be nervous as a scared cat. How'd you cure her?"*

"I just pretended to read from a paper where a doctor said nervousness was a sign of advancing age."

+

This was in church, at a men's club meeting. "What do you think of a man," whispered the inevitable gossip in such gatherings, "who will consistently deceive his wife?"

"I think," said another well-married gent, "he is obviously a genius."

Woman

Little Betsy asked, "Daddy, why do the ladies always bring their knitting when they come to visit Mommie?"

"So they will have something to think about while they talk."

One day a man dropped in at Korrick's Department Store to buy some neckties. Mr. Charles Korrick waited on him. The man tossed four or five hideous ones aside. Charlie carefully put them in a special box. "What will you do with that cast-off junk?" the customer demanded, somewhat rudely.

Charlie smiled and replied, "Raise the price and display them to women who come in to buy ties for their men."

Subject Index